PLANNING USING

PRIMAVERA PROJECT PLANNER®

P3®

VERSION 3.0

PAUL E HARRIS

DISCLAIMER

The information contained in this workbook is to the best of the author's knowledge true and correct. The author has made every effort to ensure accuracy but cannot be held responsible for any loss or damage arising from any information in this book.

AUTHOR

Paul E Harris
Eastwood Harris Pty Ltd
PO Box 4032
Doncaster Heights 3109
Victoria
Australia

Email: harrispe@eh.com.au
Tel: 61 (0)4 1118 7701
Fax: 61 (0)3 9846 7700

Please send any comments on this publication to the author.

ACKNOWLEDGEMENTS

The author would like to acknowledge D. Grant for his initial assistance supplying material which forms the basis of some chapters in this publication.

US English

16 March 2001

ISBN: 0 9577783 1 7

TABLE OF CONTENTS

1   INTRODUCTION

1.1   Purpose

The purpose of this book is to provide you with the knowledge to plan and control projects using Primavera Project Planner P3 Version 3.0. At the end of this book you will be able to:

- complete the steps to create a project plan

- set up P3 software and create a new project

- define calendars

- define activity codes

- add and organize activities

- add logic constraints and schedule

- format the display and filter activities

- print reports

- record and track progress

- modify your project and scheduling options

- create and assign resources

- understand activity types and driving resources

- status projects with resources

- understand the more advanced features of P3 and

- use project utilities.

The book does not cover every aspect of the P3 Project Planner software but covers all of the main aspects. It provides a solid grounding that allows you to learn the other features of the software from the help files and printed manuals.

The chapter entitled **WHAT'S NEW IN P3 VERSION 3.0** outlines the new features of P3 Version 3.0.

1.2 Required Background Knowledge

This book does not intend to teach you how to use computers or to manage projects. It is intended to teach you how to use P3 in a project environment. Therefore, to follow this book you should have the following background knowledge:

- the ability to use a personal computer and understand the fundamentals of the operating system,

- previous use of application software such as Microsoft Office which exposes you to the Windows menu system and functions such as copy and paste and

- an understanding of how projects are managed and the phases and processes which take place over the lifetime of a project.

1.2.1 The Purpose of Planning

The ultimate purpose of planning is to build a model that allows you to predict which **Activities** and **Resources** are critical to the timely completion of the project. This allows strategies to be implemented to ensure that these Activities and Resources are managed and to ensure that the project is delivered both "on time" and "within budget".

Planning helps to avoid:

- delays in project work

- lost revenue

- loss of facility

- additional changeover costs

- inconvenience costs

- contractual disputes and

- extensions of time claims.

Planning aims to:

- optimize time

- evaluate different methods

- optimize resources

- provide early warning of potential problems and

- take proactive, not reactive, action.

1.2.2 Project Planning Metrics

The three components that may be measured and controlled using the plan are time, cost and effort (resources).

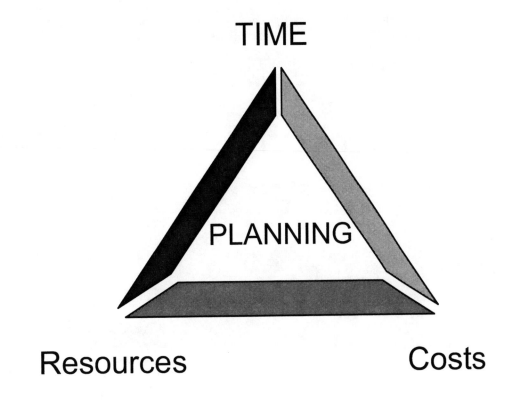

Any change in one normally results in a change in one or both of the other two.

1.2.3   Planning Cycle

The planning cycle is an integral part of managing a project. Planning software make this task much easier.

When the original plan is agreed the **Baseline** is set. The **Baseline** is therefore a record of the original plan. **Targets** is a facility in P3 to record the **Baseline dates.**

The actual progress is monitored and recorded during project execution and compared to the **Target**.

As the progress is reported and evaluated, the plan may be changed by adding or deleting activities and adjusting Remaining Durations or Resources. A revised plan is then published.

2 CREATING A PROJECT PLAN

The aim of this chapter is to give you an understanding of what a schedule is and some practical guidance on how your schedule may be created and statused as part of a project.

2.1 Understanding Planning and Scheduling Software

A project is essentially a set of operations or activities to be completed in logical order. A schedule is an attempt to model these operations and their relationships. These operations take time to accomplish and may employ resources that have limited availability.

Planning and scheduling software allows the user to:

- Break a project down into discrete activities that are entered into the software as activities.

- Nominate durations, predecessors and successors for activities and calculate the start and finish date of all the activities.

- Assign resources (which represent people, equipment or materials) to the activities and calculate the project resource requirements.

- Monitor the actual progress of activities against the original plan and amend the plan when required.

- Monitor the consumption of resources and re-estimate the resources required to finish the project.

There are four modes or levels in which planning and scheduling software may be used:

	Planning	Tracking
Without Resources	LEVEL 1 Planning without Resources.	LEVEL 2 Tracking progress without Resources.
With Resources	LEVEL 3 Planning with Resources.	LEVEL 4 Tracking progress with Resources.

As the level increases, the amount of information required to maintain the schedule will increase and, more importantly, your skill and knowledge in using the software will increase. This book is designed to take you from Level 1 to Level 4.

2.2 *Understanding your Project*

Before you start the process of creating a project plan, it is a good idea to have an understanding of the project and how it is expected to be executed. On large, complex projects this information is usually available from the following types of documents:

- Project Scope

- Requirements Analysis, Requirements Baseline

- Contract Documents

- Plans and Drawings

- Project Execution Plan

- Contracting and Purchasing plan

- Equipment Lists

- Installation Plan and

- Testing Plan.

It is important to gain a good understanding of the project process before you start to plan your project. You should also understand what level of reporting is required, as providing too little or too much detail will often lead to the schedule being discarded.

There are two processes required to create or maintain a schedule at each level:

- collecting the relevant project data and

- entering and manipulating the data in P3.

The ability to collect the data is as important as the ability to enter the information into the software. On larger projects it may be necessary to write policies and procedures to ensure accurate collection of data from the various departments and sites.

2.3 Level 1 – Planning Without Resources

This is the most simplistic mode of planning.

2.3.1 Creating Projects

To create the project you will require the following information:

- Project Name
- Client Name
- Other information such as Location and
- The Start Date (and perhaps the Finish Date).

2.3.2 Defining Calendars

Before you start entering activities into your schedule, it is advisable to set up the calendars. Calendars are used to model the working time for each activity in the project. For example, a six-day calendar is created for those activities that will be worked for six days a week. The calendars should include any public holidays and any other exceptions to available working days such as Rostered Days Off (RDO).

2.3.3 Defining Activity Codes

Activity Codes are used to sort, select, summaries and group activities. Before creating a dictionary of valid Activity Codes ask the following types of questions:

- How many phases are there? Eg Design, Procure, Install and Test.
- How many disciplines are there? Eg Civil, Mechanical and Electrical.
- Which departments are involved in the project? Eg Sales, Procurement and Installation.
- What work is expected to be contracted out?
- How many sites or areas are there in the project?

Use the response to these questions to create the Activity Codes Dictionary.

2.3.4 Adding and Organizing Activities

Activities must be defined before they are entered into the schedule. It is important that you carefully consider:

- the scope of the activity
- how long the activity is going to take
- who is going to do it and
- the deliverable for each activity.

The project estimate is usually a good place to start looking for a breakdown of the project into tasks and it may give an indication of how long the work will take.

Usually project reports are created on a regular basis, such as every week or every month. Good practice says that an activity should not span more than two reporting periods. That way the activities should only be "In Progress" for one period. An activity has slipped if it is "In-Progress" for more than two reporting periods.

It is also good practice to have a measurable finish point for each group of activities. The issue of documentation to mark the end of one task and the start point of another adds to the clarity of a schedule. Examples of document issues are:

- Issue of a Drawing Package

- Completion of a Specification

- Placing of an Order

- Delivery Dockets or

- Testing Certificates for Equipment.

The activities are then added to the schedule and assigned their Activity Codes so that they may be sorted and grouped.

2.3.5   Adding the Logic

The logic is then added to provide the order in which the activities must be undertaken and when the software schedules it will calculate the start and finish dates for each activity.

It is good practice to create a **Closed Network** with the logic. In a **Closed Network** all activities have one or more predecessors and one or more successors except:

- the project start milestone or first activity that has no predecessors and

- the finish milestone or finish activity that has no successors.

Thus when the logic is correctly applied, a delay to an activity will delay all successor activities and the project end date when there is insufficient spare time or **Float** to accommodate the delay.

To correctly model the impact of events outside of the logical sequence, you may use constraints to nominate specific dates such as the availability of a facility. Constraints should be cross-referenced to the supporting documentation.

2.3.6 Scheduling the Project

The computer will calculate the shortest time in which the project may be completed.

It will also identify the **Critical Path(s)**. The Critical Path is the chain(s) of activities that take the longest time to accomplish and this will define the earliest finish date of the project. The calculated completion date depends on the critical activities starting and finishing on time – if they are delayed, the whole project will be delayed.

Activities that may be delayed without affecting the project end date have **Float**.

Total Float is the amount of time an activity may be delayed without delaying the project end date.

Free Float is the amount of time an activity may be delayed without delaying the start date of another activity. The calculated project end date is only as accurate as the information used to derive it.

2.3.7 Formatting the Display – Filters and Layouts

Filters and Layouts are tools used to manipulate and display the activities to suit the project reporting requirements.

2.3.8 Printing and Reports

There are facilities that allow you to present the information in a clear and concise manner so as to communicate the requirements to all project members.

2.3.9 Issuing the Plan

All members of the project team should review the project plan in an attempt to optimize the process and methods employed.

Use the flexible reporting to communicate what is expected of each team member while providing them with the opportunity to further improve the outcome.

2.4 Level 2 – Monitoring Progress without Resources

2.4.1 Setting the Target Schedule

The optimized and agreed plan is used as a baseline for future comparisons. The software can record the original planned dates for comparison against actual progress during the project.

2.4.2 Tracking Progress

The schedule should be **Statused** (updated) on a regular basis and progress recorded at that point in time. The date on which progress is reported is known as the **Data Date**. Whatever the frequency chosen for statusing, you will have to collect the following activity information in order to status a schedule:

- actual start dates, percentage complete and remaining duration of in progress activities
- actual and finish dates for completed activities and
- any revisions to activities that have not started.

The schedule may be statused when this information has been collected and the recorded progress compared to the original schedule.

At this point in time it may be necessary to further optimize the schedule.

2.5   Level 3 – Scheduling with Resources

2.5.1   Creating and Using Resources

A resource pool is established by entering the project resources into the software. You then assign the required quantity of each resource to the activities.

Entering a cost rate for each resource enables you to conduct cost analysis such as comparing the cost of supplementing overloaded resources against the cost of extending the project deadline.

Time-phased cash flows and budgets may be automatically produced from this resource/cost data.

2.5.2   Activity Types and Driving Resources

These are additional features that enable the user to more accurately model real life situations.

2.6   Level 4 – Monitoring Progress of a Resourced Schedule

2.6.1   Statusing Projects with Resources

When you status a project with resources you will need to collect some additional information:

- The quantities or costs spent to date per activity for each resource.

- The quantities or costs required per resource to complete each activity.

With this data, you may then status the resourced schedule.

2.7   Additional Features

2.7.1   Tools and Techniques for Scheduling

At this point the book covers some additional scheduling techniques.

2.7.2   Project Groups and Project Utilities

Project Groups is a facility that allows you to share resources over more than one project.

Project Utilities are administration tools. These are covered last.

3   CREATING PROJECTS AND SETTING UP THE SOFTWARE

This chapter covers the following topics:

- understanding the P3 file structure
- creating new projects
- opening project files
- understanding the screen and
- customizing the screen.

There are two methods of creating a new project in P3:

- Using the **File**, **New** menu option to create a new project.
- Using **Tools**, **Project Utilities**, **Copy** to copy an existing project, opening it with **File**, **Open** and modifying it.

The method of copying projects will be covered in the **TRACKING PROGRESS** chapter.

Before creating a project file you must understand a little about the P3 file structure.

3.1   P3 File Structure

P3 will work with one file type only, **P3**, which is the standard format for P3 files:

- The project has a mandatory four characters for the project name
- A number of files are created in the project directory for each project
- All files will have a P3 file extension and
- All files are prefixed with the four character **Project name**.

When a new project is created in P3 it automatically becomes a **Project Group**. Sub projects may then be created under a project group and these sub projects are termed **Projects**. **Projects** (sometimes referred to as **Member Projects**) share the calendars, codes, resources and other data from the **Project Group**. You may work entirely within a **Project Group** and do not have to create a **Project** under a **Project Group**.

3.2 Creating a New Project

After starting P3, select **File**, **New** to create a new project. The **Add a New Project** form contains important set-up information for the calendars as well as setting defaults such as the folder location to save the project, the project name and company name.

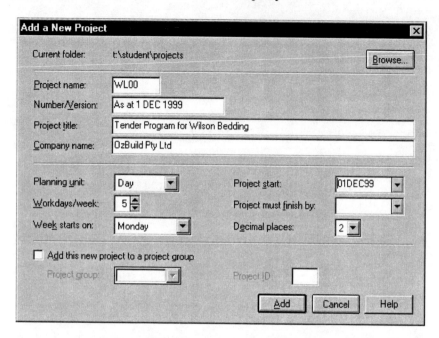

- Use **Browse** to select the folder into which your **Project Group** and/or **Project** will be saved.

- **Number/Version** is a description and is displayed when selecting **File**, **Open**.

- **Project name** must be a 4 character alpha numeric.

- **Project title** is displayed in the **File**, **Open** form and may be referenced in printed reports.

- **Company name** this is a text field only, which may be referenced in printed reports.

- **Planning unit** may be Hours, Days, Weeks or Months and cannot easily be changed in P3 once a project is created. Projects are usually created in days except where the project is of a short duration, such as close down operations where hours are used.

- **Workdays/week**, this option allows you to select the standard number of workdays per week in your project. The number of days nominated is used when the P3 calendar file is created.

- **Week starts on** is the day that is displayed on the time scale above the bar chart and is usually Monday.

- **Project start**, no activities will be scheduled before this date.

- **Project must finish by** is an optional field. This imposes a late finish date on the project. Total float is calculated to this date when a date is nominated.

- **Decimal places** allows you to nominate zero or two places when calculating resource cost information. It is suggested that you should initially select two decimal places.

- **Add this new project to a project group** allows you to create a new **Project** as "subproject" of an existing **Project Group**. You will be required to nominate a two-character code beginning with a letter that is used to identify the sub-project. This two letters become the first two characters of the code which is used to identify each activity, and is called the **Activity ID**. This topic is covered in more detail in the **PROJECT GROUPS** chapter.

- **Add** creates the new project.

You may modify the data entered in the **Add a New Project** form by selecting **File**, **Project Overview**.

 SureTrak may be used to change a project from daily to hourly or from hourly to daily.

3.3 Opening an Existing Project

Up to four files may be open at a time in P3. To open an existing schedule select **File**, **Open** or **Ctrl O**:

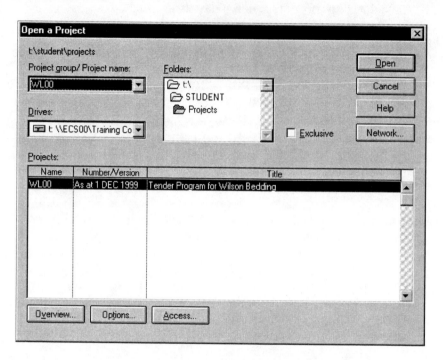

- Use **Folders** and **Drives** to select the Drive and Folder to read the project file.

- Select the existing project you wish to open by scrolling down in the drop down box under **Project group/Project name** or scrolling down in the list under **Projects**.

- **Overview** displays and allows you to edit the information entered when you created the project.

- **Options** allows you to select the layout and filter to be applied when opening the project. **Layouts** are used to organize and display the activities on the screen and **Filters** are used to select which activities will be displayed.

- Check the **Exclusive** box otherwise you will not be able to alter data such as the Activity ID.

- **Open** opens the project.

- **Access** is discussed in the next paragraph.

3.4 Operating In a Multi-user Environment

The book does not cover the multi-user environment in detail but the following are important points you must understand and are relevant when you are NOT in a multi-user environment:

- Click on the **Access** button to open the **Project Access** form which is used to nominate who may open and edit the project.

- In the **Access** form there is a **Restrictions** option and this is used to define what each user who is assigned **Restricted Access** may change.

- **Exclusive**. Certain functions, such as changing Activity IDs, scheduling and leveling may only be performed when one person has **Exclusive** access to a project. Check this box to obtain exclusive access.

- Network administration, including adding users and changing user passwords, is undertaken in a program called **Primavera Network Administration** by running the file **P3NET.EXE** found in the P3progs subdirectory. The default password for P3NET.EXE is **netset**.

 Always check the **Exclusive** box as it allows you to change the Activity ID's after an activity has been created.

WORKSHOP 1

Creating Our Project

Preamble

You are an employee of OzBuild Pty Ltd and are responsible for planning the tender preparation required to ensure a response to an RFP (Request for Proposal) from Wilson Bedding is submitted on time.

While short listed, you have been advised that the RFP will not be available prior to 1st December 1999.

Assignment

1. Create the project using the information below.

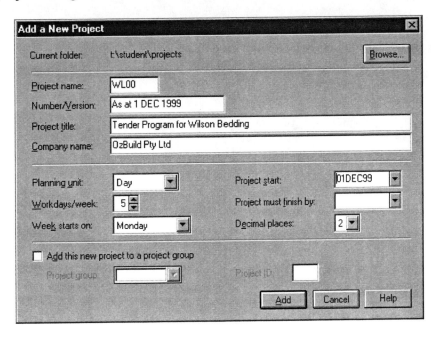

2. Click on **Add** when you have entered the data.
3. Press Esc after the **Add New Project** form closes.
4. Close your project and then open it clicking the **Exclusive** box.

3.5 The Screen

To open an existing project select **File**, **Open**. After opening the APEX project group shipped with P3 the screen will look like this:

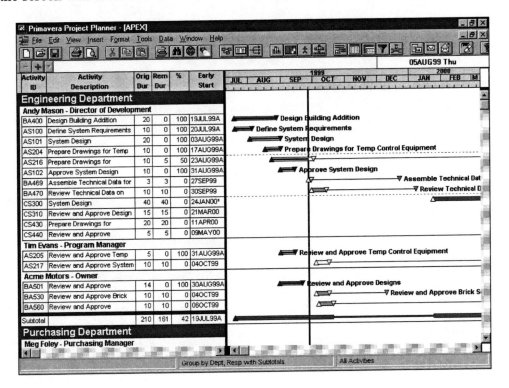

P3 has a windows menu system with a typical Windows look and feel:.

- The project name is displayed in brackets at the top of the screen.

- The drop-down menus are just below. The menus are similar to other Microsoft Windows compatible software.

- There is one toolbar below the menu. This may be displayed or hidden using the command **View**, **Toolbar** and may be edited using **Tools**, **Options**, **Toolbar.**

- To the right and below of the toolbar is the **Datometer**, this indicates the date on which the mouse is pointing when it is over the bar chart area.

- On the left-hand side below the toolbar you will find the **Edit bar**. This is where data is edited when it is selected in the column area. The 🔳 and 🔳 buttons are used for adding and deleting activities.

- The main display has the Bar Chart on the right hand side and the Data Columns on the left-hand side, with their titles above them.

- The **Activity Form** is the area at the bottom of the screen and may be displayed or hidden by pressing **F7** or **View**, **Activity Form**.

- At the bottom of the window is the **Status Bar**. This indicates the current **Layout** and current **Filter**.

WORKSHOP 2

Setting your Project Options

Preamble

We wish to get accustomed to the functions available in Primavera Project Planner.

Assignment

1. Open the APEX project from the projects directory.
2. Swap between projects using the **Window** option in the drop-down menus.
3. Hide and the re-display the **Tool Bar**.
4. Open and close the **Activity Form**.
5. Move the mouse over the bar chart area and note the change in dates in the **Datometer**.

4   DEFINING CALENDARS

The end date of an activity is calculated from the start date plus the duration over the calendar associated with the activity. Therefore, a five working day activity that starts on a Wednesday and is associated with a five day work week calendar, with Saturday and Sunday defined as the non work days, will finish on the following Tuesday.

P3 requires that all durations within a Project Group are entered using the same planning unit which was defined in the **Add a new Project** form when the project was created. The planning unit may be one of the following:

- Hours
- Days
- Weeks or
- Months.

A P3 Project Group has a **Global Calendar** and a minimum of one **Base Calendar**. The **Global Calendar** sets the default holidays for all calendars. The **Global Calendar** cannot be assigned to an activity.

Base calendars are assigned to activities. Up to 31 Base calendars may be created.

This chapter covers the following topics:

- creating daily calendars and
- creating hourly calendars.

Weekly and monthly calendars will not be covered but follow the same principles as daily calendars. They are very rarely used, so you may view them in your own time.

4.1 Daily Calendar

4.1.1 Global Calendar

Holidays nominated in the **Global Calendar** are reflected in each **Base Calendar**. The majority of projects are scheduled using daily calendars. Generally you should set a daily project **Global Calendar** to include public holidays. Public holidays on the same date every year should be made **Annual** so they appear every year. RDO's (Rostered Days Off) may also be entered here if they affect all other calendars.

When you create a project you nominate the **Workdays/week**. This entry is used to create the **Calendar 1**:

- **5 Workdays/week**, the **Global Calendar** will be a five day week calendar with Saturday and Sunday as no workdays;

- **6 Workdays/week**, the **Global Calendar** will be a six day week calendar with Sunday as a no workday;

- **7 Workdays/week**, the **Global Calendar** will be a seven day week calendar.

Select **Data**, **Calendars** to open the **Calendar** form to edit, delete or create base calendars:

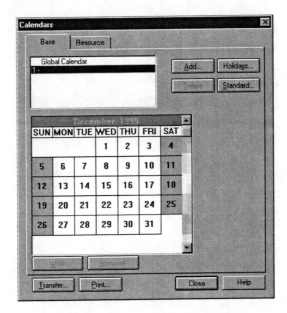

- **Add** allows you to create a new calendar, you give it a letter or number and a description.

- **Delete** allows you to delete any calendars except the **Global Calendar** and **Calendar 1**.

- **Transfer** allows you to copy a calendar within a project or copy calendars from another project into the current project.

- Double click on individual days of the week or highlight the day or click on **Work** or **Nonwork** to make the days working or non-working.

- Double Click on a day of week to highlight a column and click on **Nonwork** or **Work** to make every occurrence of that week day in that month only a work or non-workday.

- Use Windows functions such as Shift and "drag" to select a range or Ctrl to select non-consecutive days and then click on **Nonwork** or **Work**.

- **Holidays** opens the **Holiday List** form.

- **Standard** opens the **Standard Global Information** form.

- **Print** allows you to print a summary or detailed calendar report.

4.1.2 Holiday List Form

Holidays, click on this button to open the **Holidays List** form which allows you to set the holidays in the **Global Calendar**. These are reflected in all other calendars and may be overriden in the other calendars.

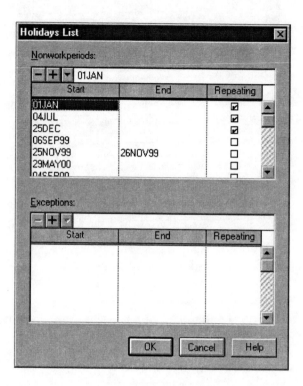

- **Nonwork periods** is used to specify holidays which may be a single day or span a period.

- **Repeating** makes the day a holiday/exception every year.

- **Exceptions** are used to make a day, that by the calendar definitions should be a non-work day, a work day.

4.1.3 Standard Global Information Form

Standard – clicking on this icon opens the **Standard Global Information** form and allows you to set certain calendar defaults.

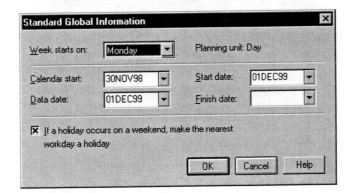

- **Week starts on** is the day the workweek commences. It is the day of the week displayed in the timescale. It was nominated when the project was created and the day may be edited here.

- **Calendar start** is the date the calendar commences and must be before the project start date.

- **Start date** is the project start date that was nominated when the project was created and may be edited here.

- **Finish date** is the nominated project finish date entered when the project was created and may be edited here. This is an optional field.

- **If a holiday occurs on a weekend, make the nearest work day a holiday** should be checked if your project staff are entitled to an additional holiday during the work week when a holiday occurs on a weekend.

4.1.4   Daily Base Calendars

Click on a **Base Calendar** listed below the **Global Calendar** to edit it.

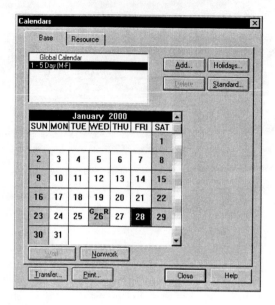

- The example above shows how the **Global Repeating** holidays are displayed in Base Calendar 1, see 26 Jan 2000.

- **Add**, **Delete**, **Holidays Transfer** and **Print** work in the same way as when you have selected the **Global Calendar**.

- Double click, **Work** and **Nonwork**, Drag, Shift and Ctrl also function in the same way as they did in **Global Calendar**.

- **Holidays** also allow you to override or add additional holidays to the **Global Calendar**.

- **Standard** allows you to specify the workdays and edit the title of the calendar. The grayed-out text **Use base calendar standard workweek** is displayed and used when editing resource calendars.

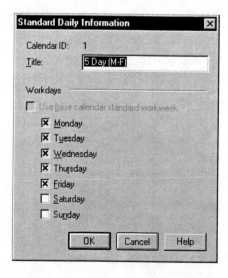

4.2 Hourly Calendars

Hourly calendars work in a similar way to the daily calendar but have the additional option of nominating work hours.

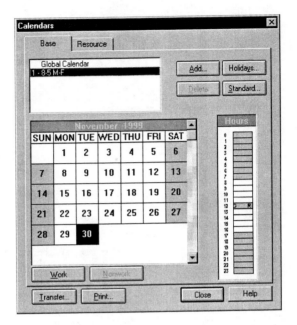

- **Add**, **Delete** and **Transfer** work in the same way as in daily calendars.

- Double click, **Work** and **Nonwork**, Drag, Shift and Ctrl also function in the same way as with **Global Calendar**.

- **Holidays** opens the **Holidays** form. This has both the day and time for the start and end of the holiday.

- **Standard** opens the **Standard Global Information** form. It has both the day and time for the calendar options.

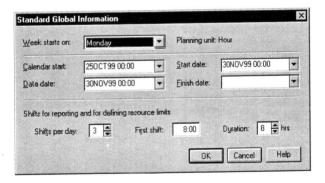

- **Shifts for reporting and for defining resource limits** is not used in schedule calculations but only for reporting resource requirements in multi-shift operations.

- Days and hours may be highlighted and made work and non-work by clicking on the **Work** and **Nonwork** buttons.

4.3 Examples of Base Calendars

Up to 31 Base Calendars may be created and assigned to activities. Examples of other calendars are:

- 2 – Weekend only
- 3 – Three Shift/24hour per day
- 4 – Mon to Thu
- 5 – Day Week
- 6 – Day Week
- 7 – Day Week.

4.4 Resource Calendars

Individual Resources may be allocated a base calendar and the resource calendar edited to reflect the availability of the resource. This facility is covered in the **CREATING AND USING RESOURCES** chapter.

When it is intended to open a SureTrak schedule in P3 then an 8-hour day calendar should be selected in SureTrak. This is because the task durations are divided by 8 when the project is opened in P3. If a project has a 10-hour day and is opened in P3, the durations will be increased by 25%.

WORKSHOP 3

Maintaining the Calendars

Preamble

The normal working week at OzBuild Pty Ltd is Monday to Friday, excluding Public Holidays. The installation staff work Monday to Saturday.

The company observes the following holidays:

Annual holidays
- New Years Day (1/1/2000) and repeating
- Australia Day (26/1/2000) and repeating
- Anzac Day (25/4) and repeating
- Christmas Day (25/12) and repeating
- Boxing Day (26/12) and repeating

Other Holidays
- Easter (21/4/2000 and 24/4/2000)
- Queen's Birthday (12/6/2000)

Assignment

1. Check the **Global Calendar** to ensure only Australian holidays are present.
2. Make the nearest workday a holiday.
3. Create calendar 5 for a five-day week and calendar 6 for the six-day week.

5   ACTIVITY CODES

Activity codes are used to sort, select, summaries and group activities under headings. They are used to present different views of your project during scheduling and statusing. These headings are often based on your Work Breakdown Structures (WBS) and Organisation Breakdown Structure (OBS).

Defining the code structure may be a major task for project managers. The establishment of templates makes this simpler as your standard codes would be predefined.

Work Breakdown Structure
Projects should be broken up into manageable areas by using a **Work Breakdown Structure** or WBS. The WBS is usually based on the various components of the project.

Organisation Breakdown Structure
Organisation Breakdown Structure is a term used to describe reporting hierarchy of people with areas of responsibility, just like an organisation chart within a company.

Other Breakdown Structures
Other common breakdown structures found are:

- Contract Breakdown Structure, allocating activities to contracts,

- System Breakdown Structure, breaking a System into Sub-Systems and Sub-Sub- Systems as used in System Engineering and

- A code structure to break a project down into physical areas.

P3 **Activity Code Dictionaries** are created for each project breakdown structure and **Activity Code Values** assigned to reflect the items within the breakdown structure. **Activity Code Values** are assigned to each activity so activities may be grouped and sorted.

5.1 Defining Activity Codes

Select **Data**, **Activity Codes** to define the Activity Codes.

P3 has two types of activity codes, **Activity codes** and **Activity ID Codes**.

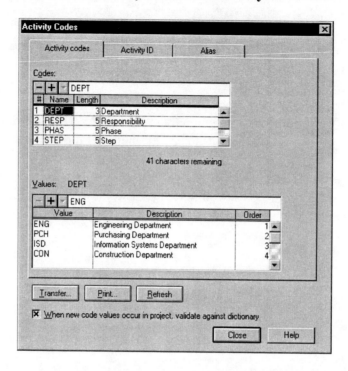

- **Activity codes** are codes are assigned to activities in the **Activity Form** or by using other methods.

- **Activity ID** codes are assigned through the logical coding of the Activity ID. These are discussed in the **ORGANISING ACTIVITIES** chapter.

- **Alias** is a facility for combining codes, this topic will be covered in the **ACTIVITY ID'S, ALIAS AND WBS CODES** chapter and may only be used in reports.

- **Transfer** allows you to transfer codes from another project.

An **Activity code** has a **Name** and a **Description**. The dictionary holds a series of **Values** and each **Value** has a **Description**.

In the example above:

- the dictionary for the Departments of the Project is named **DEPT**

- ENG is the value for the Engineering Department and

- PCH is the value for the Purchasing Department.

5.2 Creating and Deleting Code Dictionaries

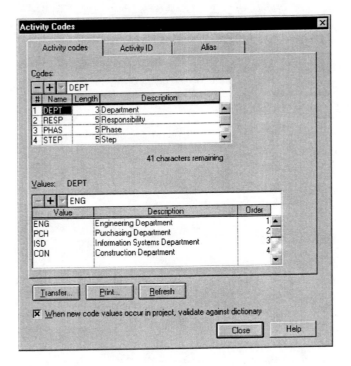

To create a new code:

- Select the place where you want to insert a new code and click ⊞ button under the title **Codes** or click into the first blank line under **Codes**.

- Give the dictionary a 1 to 4-character **Name**.

- Nominate a code **Length** to a maximum of 10 characters. The length is the maximum number of characters each code may have.

- Type in the **Description** for the code.

- To delete a dictionary, highlight the appropriate dictionary and click the ⊟ button . Deleting a dictionary will delete all the dictionary codes assigned to all activities.

- The total of all the code lengths added together has a maximum length of 64 characters.

- A maximum of 20 **Codes** are permitted.

 It is recommended to keep the code length as short as possible to reduce the number of keystrokes when assigning the code to an activity.

5.3   Creating and Deleting Activity Codes

To create a Code:

- Select a blank line or click on an existing code and click the ⊞ icon to insert a code.

- Allocate the **Code Value**. The maximum length of a **Code Value** is the code **Length** nominated in the dictionary and must be uppercase characters and numbers only.

- Type in the **Description** of the code.

- Allocate the order, from 1 to 254 to order the Codes on the screen. The lowest value is displayed at the top of the screen. If the order is not used (or has the same value) then the codes will be reordered alphabetically

- Select the ⊟ button to delete a code.

5.4   Default Activity Codes

Default activity codes may be created using **Tools, Options Default Activity Codes**. These code dictionaries are created when a new project is created. This table may be edited to suit your requirements.

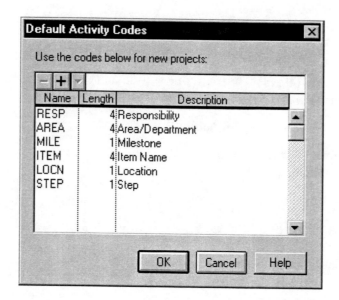

WORKSHOP 4

Maintaining the Activity Codes

Preamble

A review of the internal reporting requirements reveals that you need to identify each of the following:

        Department and they are:
                Sales
                Purchasing
                Information Technology and
                Administration.
        Person Responsible and they are:
                Angela Lowe   Purchasing
                David Williams   Account Manager
                Carol Peterson   Tender Manager
                Melinda Young   Clerical Support and
                Scott Morrison   Systems Analyst.
        and Work Phase and they are:
                Research
                Estimation and
                Proposal.

Assignment

1. In the table on the next page write down the dictionary names, lengths and descriptions and then the activity codes, values and descriptions you would create from the information above .
2. Create the activity codes using the details on the back of the next page.

FIRST CODE DICTIONARY

NAME	LENGTH	DESCRIPTION

FIRST DICTIONARY CODES

VALUE	DESCRIPTION	ORDER

SECOND CODE DICTIONARY

NAME	LENGTH	DESCRIPTION

SECOND DICTIONARY CODES

VALUE	DESCRIPTION	ORDER

THIRD CODE DICTIONARY

NAME	LENGTH	DESCRIPTION

THIRD DICTIONARY CODES

VALUE	DESCRIPTION	ORDER

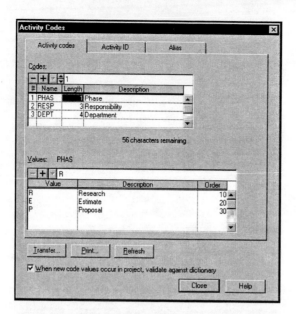

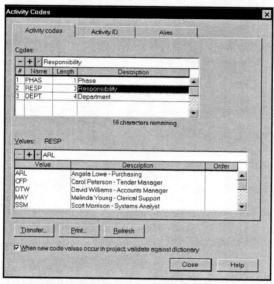

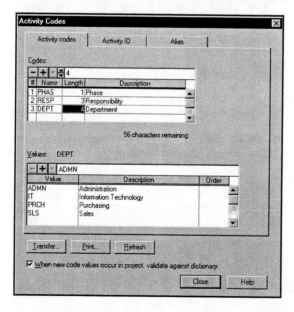

6 ADDING ACTIVITIES

This chapter looks at the methods for adding activities to your schedule.

Activities need to be well defined pieces of work with a measurable outcome. Activities such as "Slab" have confusing meanings. Does this mean form up, inspect, pour, fix reo, cure or perhaps all of these? A more appropriate activity would be "Pour Slab" or maybe "Install & Cure Slab". It also helps to repeat the code title in the activity description – ie, "Install & Cure Slab First Floor" if you have room. The limit for the descriptions is 48 characters, so try to keep the activity descriptions brief but meaningful.

6.1 Adding New Activities

There are several methods to add a task or activity.

Method 1
The first and easiest is to click on the ▣ icon found towards the top left of the screen. This will open the **Activity** form for data entry at the bottom of the screen.

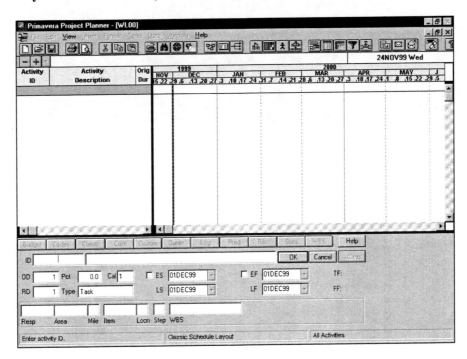

- At **ID** enter the P3 Activity ID, which may be up to 10 alpha numeric characters.

- **Tab**, and enter the description in the box to the right of the **ID** box.

- **Tab**, and enter the activity duration in the **OD (Original Duration)** box.

- **Tab**, you will be in the **RD** box (**Remaining Duration** or **Rem Dur**) and this will default to the Original Duration when it is first entered, you do not need to enter any thing at this box.

- **Tab**, at **Pct**. This is where you would enter the percent complete when statusing an activity. Do not enter anything here.

- **Tab** and enter the required Calendar ID when you do not require the default setting of Calendar 1.

- **Tab** and select the Activity **Type**. We will start with using three Task Types, **Task, Start Milestone** and **Finish Milestone.**

The other Task Types will be covered in more detail in the **USING ACTIVITY TYPES AND DRIVING RESOURCES** chapter. The other Task Type enables you to model reality more closely.

You will have then entered your first activity.

When you create your first activity, P3 does not assign an Activity ID. When you add a second activity then P3 automatically adds 10 to the previous Activity ID. To change this parameter, select **Tools, Options, Activity Inserting** to display the **Activity Inserting Options** form.

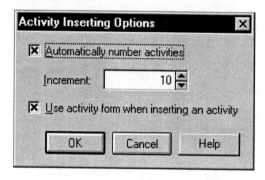

Method 2
The second method of adding an activity is to just click on the area below the existing activities.

Method 3
The third method is to select **Insert, Activity** or press the **Insert** key (Ins) on the keyboard.

6.2   Deleting Activities

To delete activities:

- Highlight the Activity or Activities you wish to delete

- Strike the **Del** (Delete) key or

- Select **Edit, Delete**.

6.3   Copying Activities in P3

Activities may be added to a project by copying from another project or copied from within the same project, using the Windows commands **Edit**, **Copy** and **Edit**, **Paste Special**.

These commands are also executed by using the menu commands **Edit Copy** and **Edit Paste** or **Ctrl C** and **Ctrl V**.

The **Paste Activities** form will be displayed to give you options for handling duplicated Activity ID's.

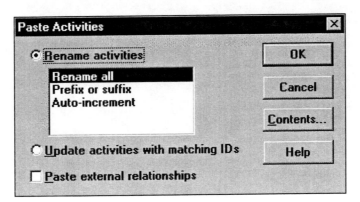

Edit, **Paste Special** gives you another option including pasting activities or objects such as pictures and text.

6.4 Copying Activities from other Programs

Activities may **NOT** be copied from other programs such as Excel by copying and pasting. The only exception is the facility to copy and paste activities to and from Primavera SureTrak.

There are several methods of copying activities from other programs. These will not be covered in detail in this chapter.

- Activities may be copied and pasted from other Windows programs into SureTrak and then copied and pasted into P3 using **Edit**, **Paste**.

- Activities may be copied and pasted into SureTrak and then the file saved in P3 format and opened in P3.

- Activities may be imported using the P3 import facility found in **Tool**, **Project Utilities**, **Import**. Files are saved in Lotus WKS or WK1 format or dBase III format. These formats may be saved from Excel.

- Primavera **Batch** facility may be used. Batch is a utility program that is not accessed through P3 and the executable file **PRMBATCH.EXE** is found in the P3PROGS directory.

WORKSHOP 5

Adding Activities

Preamble

Having set up the activity codes you may begin entering the activities.

Assignment

1. Use the **Activity Form** to enter the activities and type as detailed below:

Activity ID	Activity Description	Orig Dur	Cal ID	Act Type
1000	Tender Request Requested	0	5	Start milestone
1010	Tender Stratergy Meeting	1	5	Task
1020	Investigate Technical Feasibility	8	5	Task
1030	Document Installation Requirements	4	6	Task
1040	Request Component Tenders	3	5	Task
1050	Develop Project Schedule	4	6	Task
1060	Draft Technical Details Documents	9	5	Task
1070	Compile Costs From tenders	2	6	Task
1080	Draft Tender Documents	3	5	Task
1090	Draft tender Meeting	1	5	Task
1100	Design Presentation	1	5	Task
1110	Edit Proposal Draft	1	5	Task
1120	Finalise Tender Package	5	5	Task
1130	Final Tender Meeting	1	5	Task
1140	Submit Tender	0	5	Finish milestone

PROJECT PLANNING USING PRIMAVERA PROJECT PLANNER® P3® V3.0

7 FORMATTING THE DISPLAY

You should set up the on-screen presentation so the schedule is easy to read and consistent.

P3 has many good facilities for presenting your information.

This chapter covers the following topics:

- Toolbar
- Columns
- Formatting Bars
- Formatting Summary Bars
- Formatting Individual Bars
- Screen Colors
- Timescale
- Sightlines
- Row Height
- Fonts
- Dates
- Language
- Thousands Separator and
- Splitting the Screen.

7.1 The Toolbar

Many functions in P3 may be accessed through the toolbar. There may be some icons shown in this chapter that are not available on your toolbar, so we will start by showing you how to display and format the toolbar.

Select **View**, **Toolbar** to hide the toolbar when displayed and to display the toolbar when it is hidden.

Toolbar icons may be added or deleted by selecting **Tools**, **Options**, **Toolbar**:

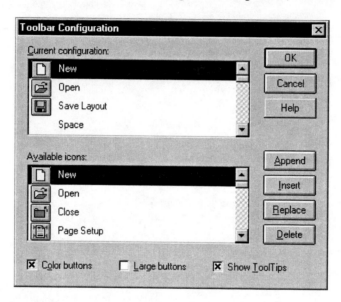

- To add Icons:
  - select the position you require the icon from the top window
  - select the icon you wish to add from the Available icons window at the bottom.
  - click **Append** to add the icon at the end of the toolbar or
  - select the location in the upper window to place the icon, the new icon will be inserted above the highlighted icon, select **Insert** to insert or **Replace** to replace the highlighted icon.

- To delete an icon, select it in the upper box and click on **Delete**.

- **Color buttons** enables the icons to be displayed in color or monochrome.

- **Large buttons** displays large or small buttons.

- **Show ToolTips** shows the icon purpose when the mouse pointer is moved on to the icon.

7.2 Formatting Columns

Formatting Columns allows you to nominate the columns you wish to see on the screen and in printouts. To open the **Columns** form:

- select **Format, Columns** or

- press **F11 Key** or

- click the 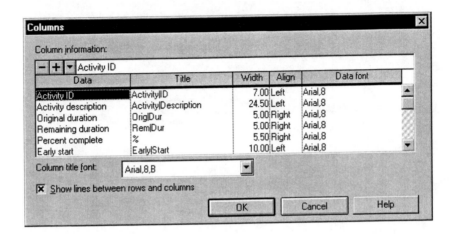 button on the toolbar.

- The columns **Data** are displayed on the screen from left to right.

- Use the ⊞ and ⊟ under **Column information** to insert or delete highlighted columns.

- The **Title** allows the displayed title to be customized.

- The column titles are formatted using the options in the **Column title font** box.

- Use the pipe symbol | (usually uppercase \) to force a new line in the title and thereby putting the title on two lines.

- Use **Width**, **Align** and **Data font** to format the data in the columns.

- Check the **Show lines between rows and columns** to display or hide lines between the columns.

- Individual columns may be formatted by double clicking on the column title in the bar view.

Activity Columns may be used to display all the resources, predecessor and successor information including the driving relationships which are indicated with a *.

Activity ID	Activity Description	Resource ID	Predecessors	Successors
1000	Tender Request Requested			1010
1010	Tender Stratergy Meeting	TM, SALESENG	1000	1020*
1020	Investigate Technical Feasibility	SYSNG	1010*	1030*, 1040, 1060*
1030	Document Installation Requirements	SCHE	1020*	1050*
1040	Request Component Tenders	SALESENG	1020	1070*
1050	Develop Project Schedule	SCHE	1030*	1080
1060	Draft Technical Details Documents	CS, LUMPSUM	1020*	1080
1070	Compile Costs From tenders	SALESENG	1040*	1080*
1080	Draft Tender Documents		1050, 1060, 1070*	1090*
1090	Draft tender Meeting		1080*	1100*, 1110*
1100	Design Presentation		1090*	1120*
1110	Edit Proposal Draft		1090*	1130
1120	Finalise Tender Package	LUMPSUM	1100*	1130*
1130	Final Tender Meeting		1110, 1120*	1140*
1140	Submit Tender		1130*	

WORKSHOP 6

Tailoring your columns

Preamble

You need to produce a report to confirm your data entry.

Assignment

1. Required fields are:
   - Activity ID
   - Description
   - Original Duration
   - Calendar and
   - Activity Type.

2. Format your columns as the picture below:

Activity ID	Activity Description	Orig Dur	Cal ID	Act Type
1000	Tender Request Requested	0	5	Start milestone
1010	Tender Stratergy Meeting	1	5	Task
1020	Investigate Technical Feasibility	8	5	Task
1030	Document Installation Requirements	4	6	Task
1040	Request Component Tenders	3	5	Task
1050	Develop Project Schedule	4	6	Task
1060	Draft Technical Details Documents	9	5	Task
1070	Compile Costs From tenders	2	6	Task
1080	Draft Tender Documents	3	5	Task
1090	Draft tender Meeting	1	5	Task
1100	Design Presentation	1	5	Task
1110	Edit Proposal Draft	1	5	Task
1120	Finalise Tender Package	5	5	Task
1130	Final Tender Meeting	1	5	Task
1140	Submit Tender	0	5	Finish milestone

Note: depending on your P3 defaults the sort order may be different.

7.3   Formatting the Bars in the Bar Chart

Select **Format**, **Bars** or click the ▦ button on the toolbar to open the **Bars** to format the bars.

The principal of this form is:

- the bars are added to the list

- they are given a description and

- then they are formatted using the **Modify Bars Definition** form and

- other bar attributes are then set in the **Bars** form.

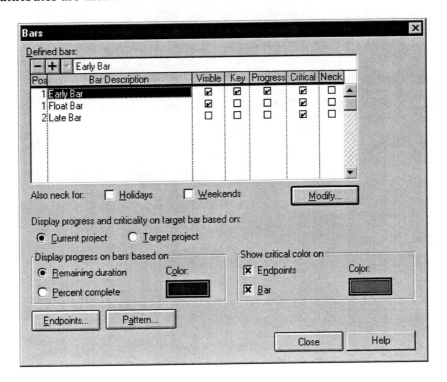

- To add a bar click in a blank line under **Defined bars** or add or delete a bar by using the ⊡ or ⊟ buttons.

- **Pos**, determines vertical placement. Position 1 is displayed above position 2. Two bars with the same position will be displayed with the bar higher up in the list laid over the bar lower in the list. This may hide the lower bar.

- The **Bar Description** may be up to 40 characters.

- Check the **Visible** box to display the bar and uncheck it to hide the bar.

- One bar may be nominated the **Key** bar. This bar is used for manipulating the activities in the Bar Chart area, such as adding logic and dragging to increase durations.

- **Progress**, box allows you display or hide the progress on the bar.

- **Critical** allows you to display critical activities in a different color.

- **Neck** displays a thinner bar during periods of inactivity, such as between **Suspend** and **Resume** dates. **Suspend** and **Resume** dates will be covered in the **TRACKING PROGRESS** chapter.

- **Also neck for** allows you to neck or show a thinner bar through weekends and/or holidays.

- **Display progress and criticality on target bar based on** allows you to display progress and criticality either on the **Current project** or on the **Target project** bars. The **Target project** is a project file that you select to compare progress against, and is usually the unprogressed original schedule.

- **Display Progress on bars based on:** has two options for displaying progress:
  - **Remaining duration** displays the **Remaining Duration** on the bar and
  - **Percent complete** displays the % Complete on the bar.
  - **Color** selects the color to highlight progress.

- **Show critical color on** allows you to display criticality on the Endpoints and/or the Bars and select the color to display criticality.

- **Modify**, **Pattern** and **Endpoints buttons** will be discussed in the following pages.

7.3.1   Defining Critical Activities

Critical activities may highlighted with a different color on bars. You may nominate in the **Critical Activities** form how much **Total Float** activities have to be critical. This is displayed by selecting **Tools**, **Options**, **Critical Activities**.

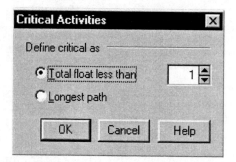

When a project schedule has multiple calendars, it is possible to have activities with float on the longest path. This occurs when the successor activity may not start immediately after the predecessor due to successor calendar Non Work periods. Thus to correctly identify critical activities when two or more calendars are used either:

- The **Longest path** should be selected or

- **Total float less than** be adjusted to compensate for calendar differences. For example when a 5 day and 7 day calendar are used the value should be set to 3.

7.3.2 Format, Bars – Modify button

After opening the bars form using **Format**, **Bars** select the bar you wish to modify by highlighting it and then clicking on the **Modify** button. This will open the **Modify Bar Definition** form.

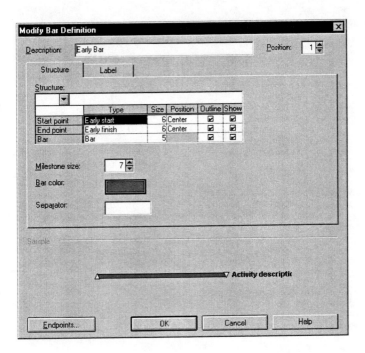

Each bar has its own **Description, Position, Structure** and **Label**. The structure and label data is accessed using the **Structure** and **Label** tabs.

Structure Tab

- The Structure tab includes options for the **Start point**, **End point** and the **Bar**.

- **Type**. The **Start point** and **End point Type** allows you to select, from a drop down list, the date fields that will define the start and finish of the bar. **Early start** and **Early finish** are most commonly used. The Target dates should be selected from the bottom of the list when you require a **Target Bar**. The Target date options appear in the list after the Target schedule has been nominated. Setting Targets will be covered in the **TRACKING PROGRESS** chapter.

- **Size** sets the height of the bar.

- **Outline** displays or hides a solid black outline.

- **Show** displays or hides the start point, end point or the bar.

- **Milestone size** sets the height of the milestones.

- **Bar color** sets the fill color of the bar.

- **Separator** allows five characters to separate any label text placed in the same position, this is used in conjunction with the **Label Tab**.

Label Tab

The Label tab allows the placement of text around the bar.

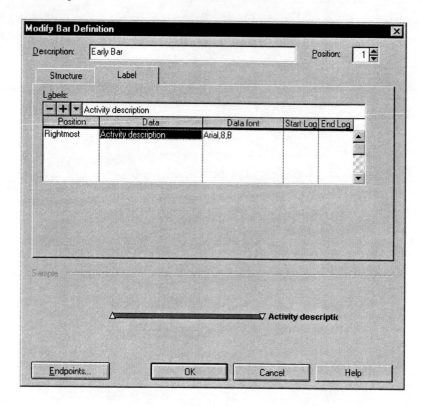

- **Position** can be one of the ten listed below:

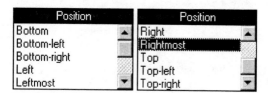

- **Data** can be any of the P3 activity fields, code values, log records or customs data items.

- **Data font** allows the data to be formatted with font size, italics and/or bolding.

- **Start log** allows control over the start of the range of log records to print.

- **End log** allows control over the end of the range of log records to print.

- **Separator** (found on the **Structure** tab) allows up to five characters to separate any label text placed in the same position.

7.3.3 Format, Bars – Pattern button

This option allows you to assign patterns to activity bars based on Activity Codes which will be covered later. **Patterns** are not covered in detail.

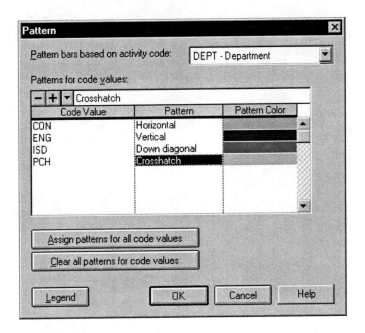

7.3.4 Format, Bars – Endpoints button

This option allows you to format the endpoints for bars.

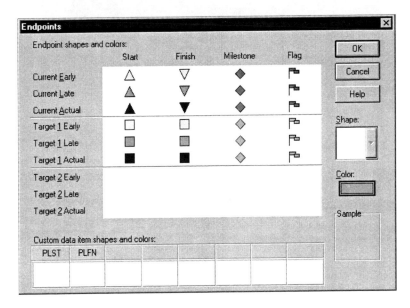

There is a program called **Endpoint Manager**. This program is accessed for outside P3 and gives you even more options for formatting the Endpoints. The program filename is **PRMENDPK.EXE**.

7.4 Format Summary Bars

The **Format**, **Summary Bars** is an option for displaying summary bars when they are created by rolling up activities when organized using **Format**, **Organize**.

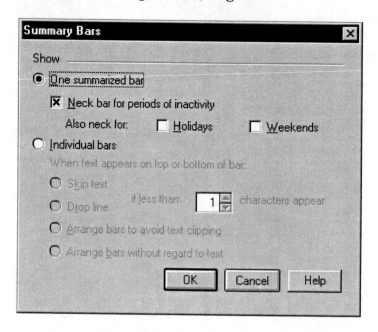

It is suggested you experiment with these when you wish to display summary bars.

7.5   *Format Individual Bars*

You may format individual bars by changing the color, bar type, endpoints and flag shapes. You may either:

- format one or more bars or

- copy that format to other bars or

- reapply the original format.

7.5.1   Format One or More Bars

To format one or more bars:

- Highlight the bar or bars you wish to format and

- Select **Format, Selected Bars, Modify Bar Format**, to open the **Format Select Bars** form:

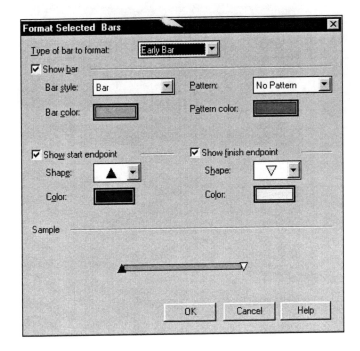

- Select the bar you wish to format from the **Type of bar to format** the drop down box at the top of the form.

- Uncheck the **Show Bar, Show start endpoint** and/or **Show finish endpoint** boxes to hide the bar, start or end points.

- Select any of the other parameters as required.

- Click **OK** to apply the formatting.

- Parameters that display **Critical** or **Progress** will overlay any individual bar formatting.

7.5.2   Copy and Paste Bar Format

Use select **Copy Bar Format** and **Paste Bar Format** to copy and paste a format from one bar to one or more bars.

7.5.3   Reapply the Original Format

Use select **Format, Selected Bars, Use Default Bars Format** to reapply the default bar format settings.

7.6   Screen Colors

The dark background with light printing is unsatisfactory on some black and white printers so you may need to choose a more acceptable screen color scheme.

Select **Format, Screen Colors** or click the 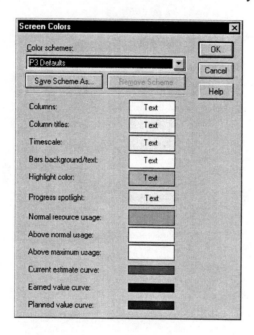 button on the toolbar to open the **Colors** form. There are some standard color schemes available to choose from or you may create your own.

7.7 Format Timescale

Format, Timescale provides a number of options for formatting the timescale displayed above the Bar Chart.

Select **Format, Timescale** or double click on the **Timescale**:

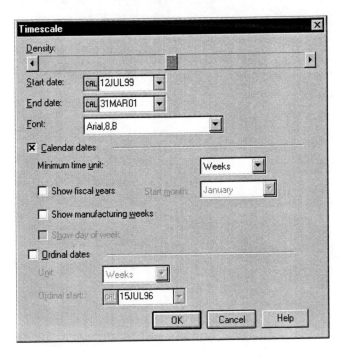

- Click on the box below **Density** and slide the box left and right to alter the scale or density of the time scale.

- **Calendar dates** is an option for displaying or not displaying the dates in the timescale.

- **Minimum time unit** is the smallest time unit to be displayed (hours, days, weeks, months, quarters or years).

- **Show fiscal years** allows accounting style years with the first month being something other than January, and is often June.

- **Show manufacturing weeks** shows week number with week one being the first week in January.

- **Show day of week** displays the day as M, T, W or Mon, Tue, Wed depending on the scale when the **Minimum time unit** is set at **Day**.

- **Ordinal dates** counts in days, weeks or months from a nominated start date selected in the **Ordinal start box**.

- The **Start date** and **End date** settings prevent the right hand boundary of the Bar Chart from scrolling outside these dates. Therefore when set correctly, it prevents you from scrolling out of the project timescale and "becoming lost" in the past or future.

Setting Start date and End date

The start and end dates may be set as either an absolute date or a **Rolling Date**. The rolling date is set as a displacement from one of the project dates. ie. the project start date, data date or end date. The advantage of using rolling dates is that as the project dates change and the start and end dates are automatically adjusted.

You should set the **Timescale** to a scale to suit your needs. A good starting point is to set the **Start date** to **Data Date -10 days** and the **End date** to **Finish Date +30 days**. Typically, the minimum time unit to display on screen is best set to a **Week**.

To set the **Start date** and **End date** of the Timescale:

- Click on the box to the left of the Start date and/or End date to select a date setting for the time scale. Select either the **Calendar date**, **Start date**, **Data date** or **End date**.

- When a **Calendar date** is selected a calendar is displayed and you may then select a date from the calendar.

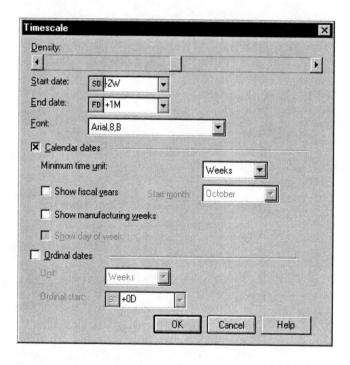

- Then enter the number of days, weeks or months in the box to the right of the **Start date** or **End date** to set the final **Start date** or **End date** position on the time scale (as in the picture above).

7.8 Format Sight Lines

Sight Lines are important to help divide the visual presentation of the dividing lines on the Bar Chart.

Select **Format**, **Sight Lines** to open the **Sight Lines** form. Use this form to format the Horizontal and Vertical Sight Lines in the Bar Chart.

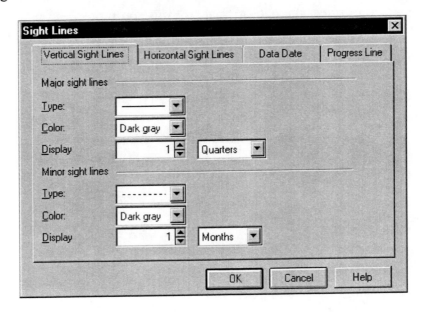

Select each tab to format the required sight lines.

 Many laser printers will not print out light gray so it is often better to use dark gray or black Sight Lines.

7.9 Format Row Height

Select **Format**, **Row Height** to open the **Row Height** form to specify the row height in the column area.

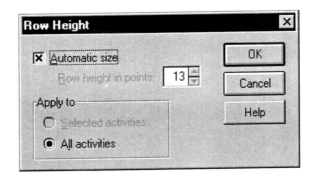

7.10 Format Fonts

Select **Format Fonts** to open the **Fonts Definition** form. This is where you specify the fonts available for selection from the drop down boxes in forms.

7.11 Format Dates

This option allows you to select the date format from the drop down box. When a separator is required between the day, month and year then this is selected from the **Separator** drop down box.

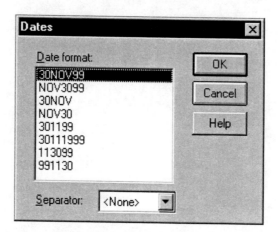

 It is recommended that you use the format at the top of the list **30NOV99** as there will be no confusion between the American (MMDDYY) date format and the European (DDMMYY) date format.

7.12 Changing Language for Column Descriptions and Timescale

Tools, **Options**, **Set Language** allows you to select a language for the column and timescale headings. Should you wish to show a task description in another language, you may enter the translated description into a **Custom Data Item**. This topic is covered in the **TOOLS AND TECHNIQUES FOR SCHEDULING** chapter.

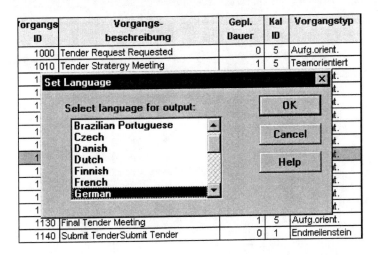

7.13 Thousands Separator

You may nominate to display or hide a thousands separator with **View**, **Thousands Separator**.

7.14 Splitting the Screen

The screen may be split into eight sections as shown below. This will enable you to scroll across and see additional columns while still displaying the activity description or two different time zones in the bar chart area.

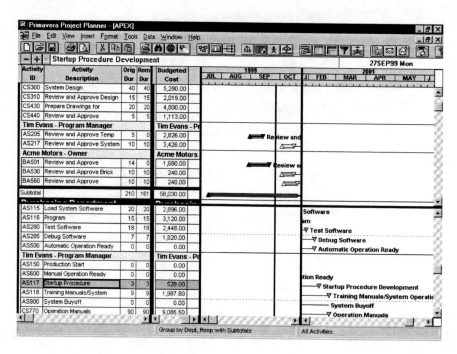

To split the screen, move the mouse to the thick black section of the scroll bar at the end of one of the scroll bar arrow icons as shown below:

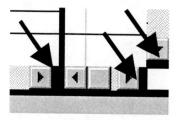

The mouse will change to a double arrow, click with the left button and drag the divider to where you want it.

WORKSHOP 7

Formatting the Bar Chart

Preamble

Management have received a draft report and requested the following changes:

Assignment

Format your project so it looks like the picture below by:

1. Press F9 to reschedule the project so the timescale functions will operate correctly.
2. Formatting the timescale to days.
3. Setting the Timescale Start date to equal Start date -1w.
4. Setting the Timescale Finish date to equal Finish date +2w.
5. Hiding the start points on the bars.
6. Placing Early start date at the left of the Early bar and Finish date at the right of the early bar.
7. Formatting Sight lines to dark gray and vertical spacing at weeks and days.
8. Splitting the screen two ways.

Activity ID	Activity Description	Orig Dur	Cal ID	Act Type	Early Start	Early Finish
1000	Tender Request Requested	0	5	Start	01DEC99	
1010	Tender Stratergy Meeting	1	5	Task	01DEC99	01DEC99
1020	Investigate Technical Feasibility	8	5	Task	01DEC99	10DEC99
1030	Document Installation	4	6	Task	01DEC99	04DEC99
1040	Request Component Tenders	3	5	Task	01DEC99	03DEC99
1050	Develop Project Schedule	4	6	Task	01DEC99	04DEC99
1060	Draft Technical Details	9	5	Task	01DEC99	13DEC99
1070	Compile Costs From tenders	2	6	Task	01DEC99	02DEC99
1080	Draft Tender Documents	3	5	Task	01DEC99	03DEC99
1090	Draft tender Meeting	1	5	Task	01DEC99	01DEC99
1100	Design Presentation	1	5	Task	01DEC99	01DEC99
1110	Edit Proposal Draft	2	5	Task	01DEC99	02DEC99
1080	Draft Tender Documents	3	5	Task	01DEC99	03DEC99
1090	Draft tender Meeting	1	5	Task	01DEC99	01DEC99
1100	Design Presentation	1	5	Task	01DEC99	01DEC99
1110	Edit Proposal Draft	2	5	Task	01DEC99	02DEC99
1120	Finalise Tender Package	6	5	Task	01DEC99	08DEC99
1130	Final Tender Meeting	1	5	Task	01DEC99	01DEC99
1140	Submit Tender	0	5	Finish		30NOV99

8   ASSIGNING ACTIVITY CODES AND ORGANISING

Activities may be grouped under their Activity Codes. This enables the activities to be grouped and presented under different headings.

Activity Codes must be assigned to activities before the activities may be grouped under their respective Codes.

The activities are then sorted under their Activity Code headings using **Organize**.

The example shows a project organized by Phase and Responsibility with some bands summarized. These have a "+" in front of the band heading.

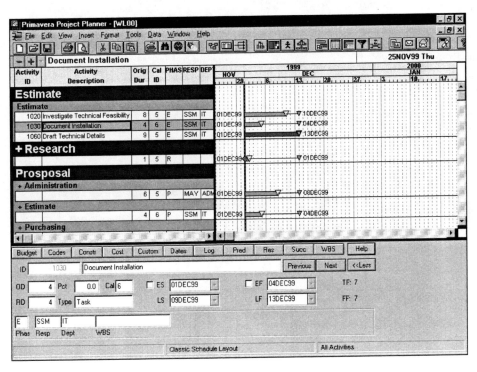

This chapter covers the following topics:

- Assigning Activity Codes to activities,

- Organizing Activities under their respective codes and

- Summarizing and Expanding Bands that are created by organizing activities under their activity codes.

8.1 Assigning Activity Codes

You may assign Activity Codes to activities as you create them or later. Activity Codes may be assigned to activities in a number ways:

- Using the Code Boxes at the bottom of the **Activity Form** (see below) or

- Creating columns for each code and assigning them using the edit box or

- Using the **Codes** form by selecting **View**, **Activity Detail**, **Codes** or **Ctl M**.

- You may also drag the activity to a new band to assign the code pertaining to that band. Click on an activity, move the mouse arrow to the left hand side of the activity and generate a double arrow mouse pointer, click and drag the activity to a new band. The activity code of the new band will be assigned to the activity.

When you type in a new code that is not contained in the Activity Code dictionary, you will be presented with a form requesting the new title. This enables the new code to be added to the dictionary while coding the activity.

When you click on an activity in a band and then create a new activity in that band, the new activity will inherit the codes of that band.

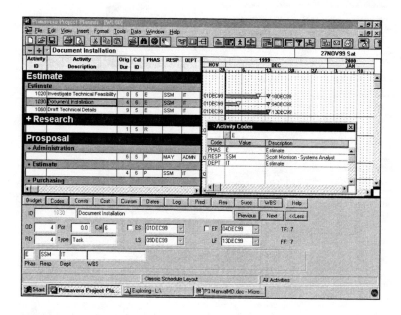

The example above shows:

- activities Grouped by Phase and Area
- the **Activity Codes** form
- the codes at the bottom left hand side of the Task Form and
- the codes displayed in columns.

WORKSHOP 8

Assigning Activity Codes

Preamble

Having entered the activities, you may now assign the codes to the activities.

Assignment

1. Format your columns to reflect details below:

Activity ID	Activity Description	Orig Dur	Cal ID	Phase	Responsibility	Department
1000	Tender Request Requested	0	5	R	CFP	SLS
1010	Tender Stratergy Meeting	1	5	R	DTW	PRCH
1020	Investigate Technical Feasibility	8	5	E	SSM	IT
1030	Document Installation	4	6	E	SSM	IT
1040	Request Component Tenders	3	5	P	ARL	PRCH
1050	Develop Project Schedule	4	6	P	SSM	IT
1060	Draft Technical Details	9	5	E	SSM	IT
1070	Compile Costs From tenders	2	6	P	ARL	PRCH
1080	Draft Tender Documents	3	5	P	DTW	PRCH
1090	Draft tender Meeting	1	5	P	CFP	SLS
1100	Design Presentation	1	5	P	DTW	PRCH
1110	Edit Proposal Draft	2	5	P	MAY	ADMN
1120	Finalise Tender Package	6	5	P	MAY	ADMN
1130	Final Tender Meeting	1	5	P	DTW	PRCH
1140	Submit Tender	0	5	P	CFP	SLS

2. Try using all of the methods to enter these codes.

8.2 Organizing Activities

Projects may be organized by Activity Codes and many other Activity Data Items such as resources, dates, float, percentages, predecessors and successors. **Reorganize automatically** will move activities under their correct group headings each time data is changed. When you are assigning Activity Codes, it is recommended that you switch this facility off so the activities do not move around as you assign their codes.

To organize activities select **Format organize** or click the 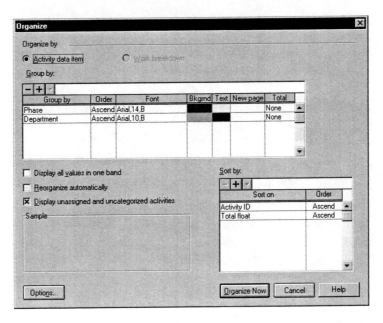 button on the toolbar:

- Select the **Activity data item** radio button at the top of the form.

- In the upper window click on the ⊡ button to create or the ⊟ button to delete a **Grouping**. Each grouping automatically produces a heading or band separating the activities that belong to this group from the others.

- Use **Order**, **Font**, **Background** and **Text** to format the headings.

- **New Page** creates a page break at each new group code when printing.

- **Total** is used to place a total at the top or bottom of a group. Values and Quantities are totaled. Dates are calculated (early dates are the earliest of the early date and the late dates are the latest of the late dates) and a summary bar produced.

- When **Reorganize automatically** is switched off you may reorganize the activities after assigning or changing Activity Codes by pressing **F5** or selecting **Format, Reorganize** or clicking the ⊞ button on the toolbar.

- **Display unassigned and uncategorized activities** displays activities without codes and are summarized under a heading **Unassigned**.

- **Sort by** is used to order the activities within bands.

8.3 Organize Options

The **Options** button in the **Organize** form displays the **Options** form.

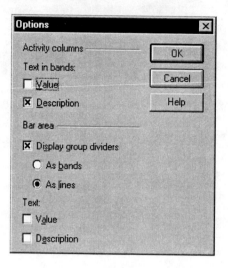

- **Text in bands**:
  - Check **Value** to display the activity code value in the group band.
  - Check **Description** to display the code description in the group band.
- **Bar area** gives you options for extending the band separators in the bar area and placing the descriptions in the bar area bands (see below).

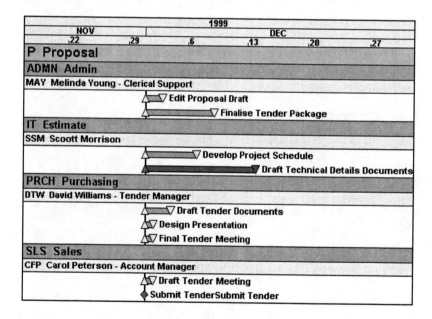

8.4 Summarizing and Expanding Bands

Bands may be summarized to a code level by selecting **Format, Summarize All**.

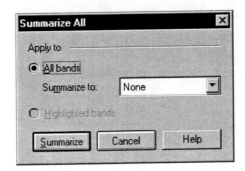

- You may apply the summarization to all bands and select the level from the drop down box or
- If you select one band then you will have the option of summarizing the highlighted band to a level.

Individual bands may also be summarized by:

- Double clicking on the band or
- Highlighting a band heading by clicking on the band heading and selecting **Format, Summarize** or
- Using the **Summarize** button ⊇– on the toolbar.

Individual bands may also be expanded by:

- Double clicking on the band or
- Highlighting a band heading by clicking on the band heading and selecting **Format, Expand** or
- Using the expand button Σ+ on the toolbar.

WORKSHOP 9

Organizing your data

Preamble

Having entered the activity codes, you may sort the activities in a different sequence.

Assignment

1. Group by Phase and sort by Activity Description.
2. Remove grouping and then group by Department, Responsibility and Phase.
3. Total the Responsibility Grouping only (place it at the top).
4. Remove all grouping and sort by Activity ID.

9   ADDING THE LOGIC

The next phase of a schedule is to add the logic to the activities. There are two types of logic that you must understand:

- The first is the logic **links or relationships** between activities and

- The second is the imposed **constraints** on the activities.

9.1   *Understanding Relationships*

There are four types of relationships available in P3; they are Finish-to-Start (**FS**) (also known as conventional), Start-to-Start (**SS**), Start-to-Finish (**SF**) and Finish-to-Finish (**FF**).

Two other terms you must understand are:

- **Predecessor**, an activity that controls the start or finish of another activity, and

- **Successor**, an activity whose start or finish depends on the start or finish of another activity.

If you were to draw a **FS** relationship (or conventional) it would look like this:

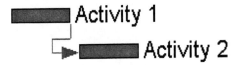   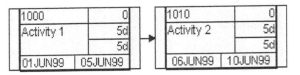

While the **SS** relationship looks like this:

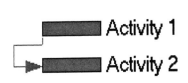   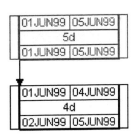

The **SF** relationship looks like:

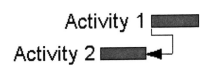   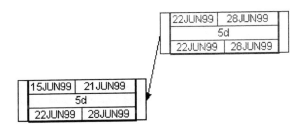

The **FF** relationship would be:

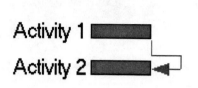
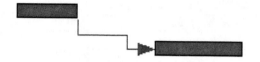
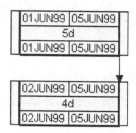

An example of a **FS** with positive lag:

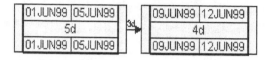

and an example with negative lag:

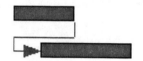
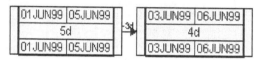

Lag is calculated on the predecessor's calendar.

 You must be careful when using a lag to allow for delays such as curing concrete when the predecessor is not a seven-day calendar. The concrete will cure while the predecessor calendar has non-work days.

9.2 Adding Relationships to the Activities

There are a number of methods for adding logic to activities. This chapter will look at the following techniques:

- Graphical adding, editing and deleting relationships,

- Series Link and Unlink,

- Successor and Predecessor forms and

- PERT View.

9.2.1   Graphical Adding, Editing and Deleting Relationships

Adding Relationships

There are two modes of screen presentation. The first is where links are displayed on the screen. The second is without links. When links are shown, logic may be added on the screen using the mouse. To change between modes click on the ⊞ button in the tool bar, push **F3** or select **View**, **Relationships**.

You may add relationships on the screen by right clicking on the end of the predecessor activity bar, the mouse arrow is replaced by a ⭗, hold down the mouse button and dragging to the start of the successor activity.

To create other relationships such as **Start to Start**, drag from the beginning of the predecessor to the beginning of the successor bar.

Editing Relationships in the Bar Chart View

Click on a relationship line and this will open the **Edit Relationship** form. This allows you to select and edit a relationship.

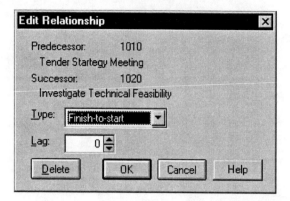

The **Confirm Relationships** form will be displayed when there is more than one relationship line and you are able to select the relationship you wish to edit.

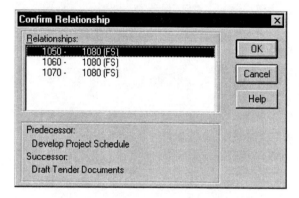

You may also select an activity and select **Edit, Relationships** to open the **Select Relationship** form.

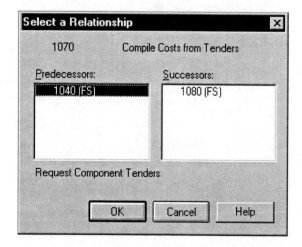

9.2.2 Link and Unlink

The Series Link is a method of linking a series of activities with **Finish to Start** relationships.

- highlight the activities to be linked and
- click **Edit**, **Link Activities** or the ⬛ button on the tool bar,
- now all the activities are linked.

The activities need not be consecutive activities to be **Linked**. Activities may be selected at random with the **Ctrl** key held down and then **Linked**. When activities lower down in the schedule are selected first, they will not be linked in the order they were selected. Activities will be linked from top to bottom.

To remove Finish to Start relationships, select the activities to be unlinked and use:
- the ⬛ button on the tool bar or
- select **Edit**, **Unlink**.

9.2.3 Autolink

The **Autolink** facility automatically assigns a Finish to Start relationship to an activity you highlight before adding an activity.

Select **Insert**, **Autolink** to turn this facility on or off.

9.3 Deleting Relationships

Relationships may be deleted by

- Opening the **Predecessor or Successor** form.

- Clicking on a Relationship Line on the Bar Chart to display the **Edit Relationship** form.

- Using **Series Unlink** as described above

- Highlight an activity and select **Edit, Relationships** to open the **Edit a Relationship** form.

- Highlight one activity and select **Edit, Extract Activity,** this will join all predecessor activities to the successor activities of the highlighted activity and remove all predecessors and successors from the highlighted activity.

- Highlight one activity and select **Edit, Dissolve Activity,** this will join all predecessor activities to the successor activities of the highlighted activity and delete the highlighted activity.

9.3.1 Successor and Predecessor Forms

The third way to link activities is to use the **Successor** and/or the **Predecessor** forms. There are several methods of opening these forms.

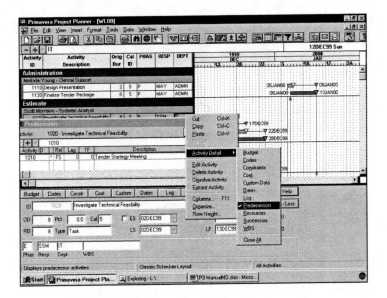

- Highlight the activity and click the right mouse button, which causes a pop-up menu to appear. Then select **Activity Detail**, a sub-menu pops up from which you may select the required form. The Predecessor Form is shown below.

- Select **View**, **Activity Detail** which shows the same menu opened by the right mouse button.

- Click on the Pred and/or Succ in the **Activity Form**.

- Click on the Predecessor or Successor Tool Bar Icons.

- Use the Pert View (which will be covered next).

When the form is open, you may insert the relationships required, including the link type and the lag.

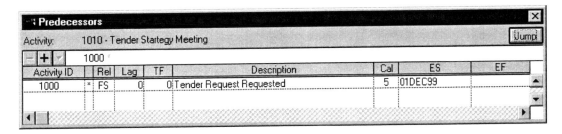

Scroll right to display a substantial amount of information on the activity.

Jump is used to move to the highlighted predecessor or successor.

9.4 PERT View

Select **View PERT** or press F6 or click on the 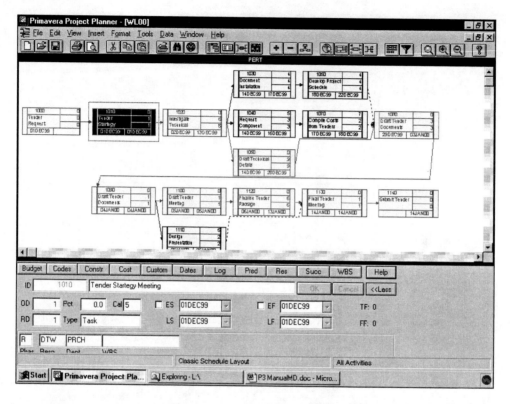 icon. The screen will change from **Bar Chart** view to **PERT** view.

Position the mouse on the left (for start) or right (for finish) end of the predecessor activity, waiting for the cursor to change to a ⌇ then drag (ie hold the left mouse button down) the cursor to the left or right of the successor activity bar.

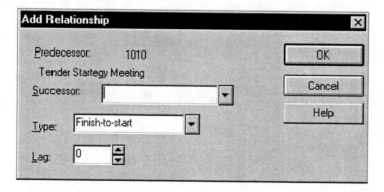

When the activity is not visible release the mouse in a blank area and choose the successor using the **Successor Activity** form.

To change the relationship or alter the lag on an existing relationship, move the mouse over the relationship line and left click to open the **Edit Relationship** form.

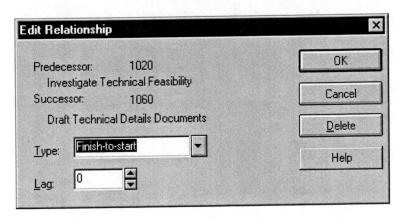

9.4.1 Formatting your PERT View

Select **Format**, **Relationship** as the first step in tailoring the PERT view.

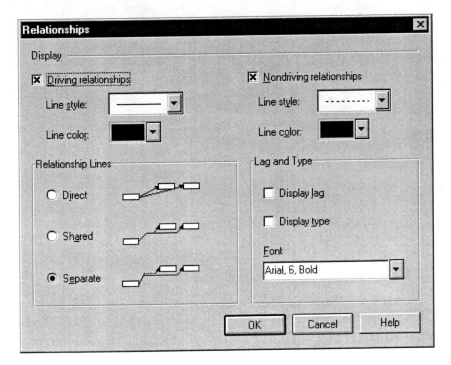

This allows you to choose:

- To display/not display the driving and non-driving relationships
- Change the color and line style
- Change to method of drawing the relationship lines and
- Display the lag and relationship type in the font of your choice.

Select **Format**, **Activity Box Configuration** to open the **Activity Box Configuration** form as the next step in tailoring the PERT view.

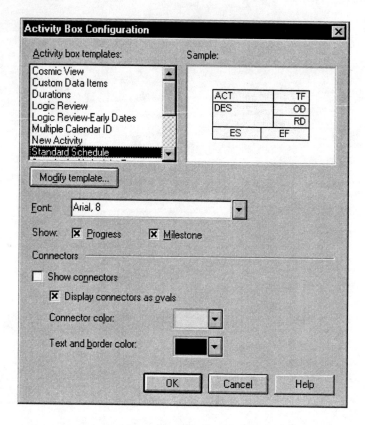

This allows you to:

- select/modify the contents of each activity box

- select the font to be used for the text in the box

- display/not display connectors not in your current view

- configure the connectors fill and text/border color or

- optionally indicate progress and milestones.

Modifying/creating a new template by using the **Modify** template button to open the **Modify Template** form:

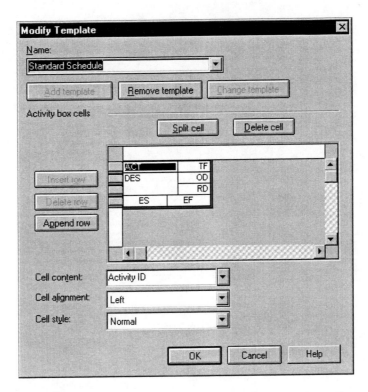

Entering a new template name activates the **Add template** button and allows you to store your modifications under a new name.

Select the cell you wish to modify and then either:

- alter the cell contents, alignment or style

- insert a row above the row of that cell

- delete the row of that cell

- append a row to the last row of the box

- split the selected cell in two or

- delete the cell but leave the row and other cells in that row.

Select **Format, Activity Box Ends and Colors** to open the **Activity Box Ends** form as the next step in tailoring the PERT view.

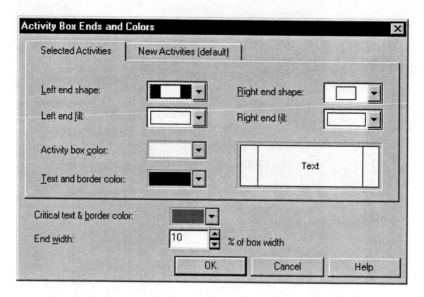

You may tailor the shape, pattern, color and width of the ends of the boxes. Use a filter or the **Shift/Ctrl** keys to select multiple activities you wish to format.

9.4.2 Timescale PERT

A timescaled Pert is available which presents the activities with a timescale.

From the Pert view select **Format, Organize** to open the **Organize** form and select the **Arrangement** tab.

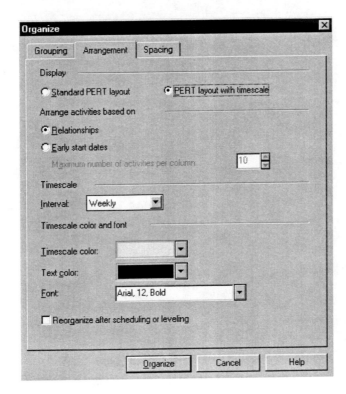

- You may select the **Standard PERT layout** or the **PERT layout with timescale** (see the next page for an example).

Standard PERT layout

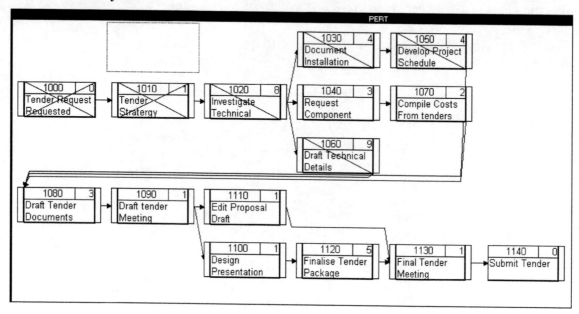

PERT layout with timescale

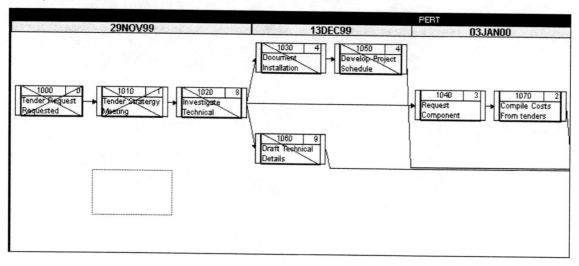

WORKSHOP 10

Adding the relationships

Preamble

You have determined the logical sequence of activities so you may now create the relationships.

Assignment

1. Input the logic below using the different methods covered in this chapter

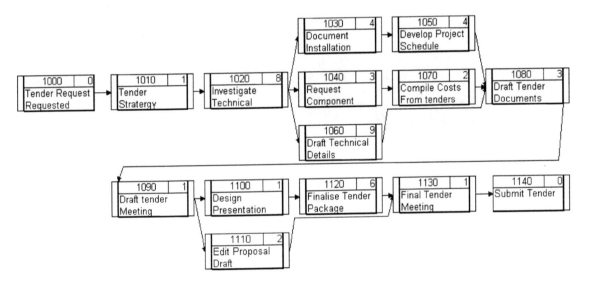

2. Format the PERT diagram to reflect the layout above.

Hint: select **Format**, **Activity Box Configuration**, and select **New Activity** under **Activity box templates** to alter the contents of the Activity Boxes.

9.5 Scheduling the Project

Now that you have activities and logic in place, it is time to calculate the activity dates. More specifically, you will **Schedule** the project to calculate the Early Dates, Late Dates and the Float. This will allow you to determine the **Critical Path** of the project.

There are three methods to calculate the schedule:

- Select **Tools**, **Schedule**, check the **Data date** is correct, click on the [Schedule Now] button and then P3 will present you the **Output Options** form with options for viewing or saving a text **Scheduling Report**.

- If you know that the **Data date** is correct, then you may simply press **F9** to schedule the project and you will not be presented with a scheduling report.

- Click on the Tool Bar icon ⊛.

It is also possible to have the **Automatic Scheduling** option switched on so the software reschedules every time you make a change to the data. This is found under **Tools**, **Schedule**, **Options**.

Understanding Tools, Schedule
Select **Tools**, **Schedule** and check that the **Data date** is correct.

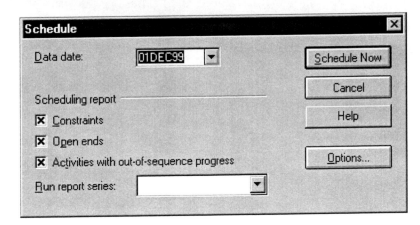

- The **Options** form has advanced options for scheduling and will be discussed in the **SCHEDULING OPTIONS AND OUT OF SEQUENCE PROGRESS** chapter.

- The options under **Scheduling report** allow you to reduce the size of the text scheduling report.

- Press the **Enter** key or click the **Schedule Now** button to schedule.

P3 will then present you with options for handling the **Scheduling Report**.

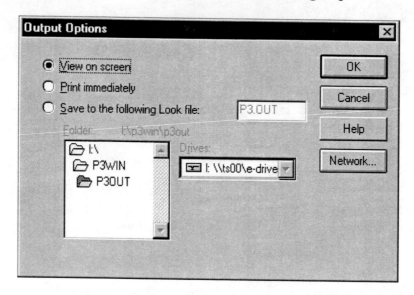

You may either:

- **View on screen** and the report will be displayed on the screen utilizing a program called **P3 Look**, the Primavera text editor. You may review the report in P3 Look and close the program down by selecting **File**, **Close** or clicking on the top right hand corner of the screen or

- **Print immediately** and the report will be sent to the printer or

- **Save to the following Look file** and save the report as a text file.

 If you are involved in managing a complex project schedule then you must study and understand the **Scheduling Report**. It contains valuable and important information and will highlight potential problems in your project.

To help understand the calculation of late and early dates, float and critical path, we will now manually work through an example. The boxes below represent activities.

ES = Early Start   EF = Early Finish

         DUR = Duration

LS = Late Start   LF = Late Finish

ES	EF
DUR	
LS	LF

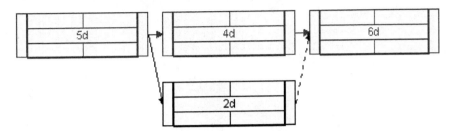

Forward Pass

The forward pass calculates the early dates. $EF = ES + DUR - 1$

Start the calculation from the first activity and work forward in time.

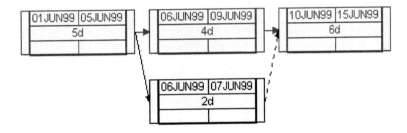

Backward Pass

The backward pass calculates the late dates. $LS = LF - DUR + 1$

Start the calculation at the last activity and work backwards in time.

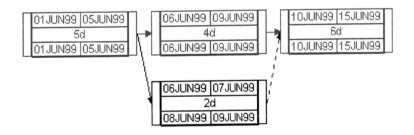

Note, the critical path is the path where any delay causes a delay in the project.

The solid relationship lines represent **Driving Relationships**, whereas the broken relationship lines represent **Non-Driving Relationships**.

Float is the difference between the **Late Finish** minus **Early Finish**. The 2 day activity has float of $9 - 7 = 2$. None of the other activities have float.

WORKSHOP 11

Scheduling Calculations

Assignment

1. Schedule your project by pressing F9 and note the end date.
2. Calculate the early and late dates for the following activities assuming a Monday to Friday working week.

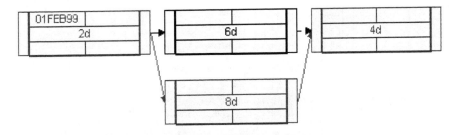

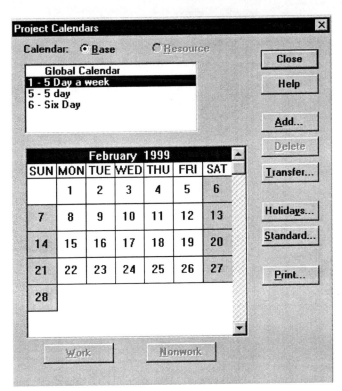

ANSWER

Forward Pass $EF = ES + DUR - 1$

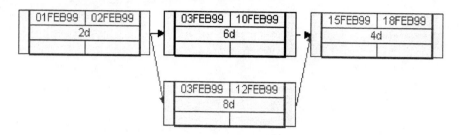

Backward Pass $LS = LF - DUR + 1$

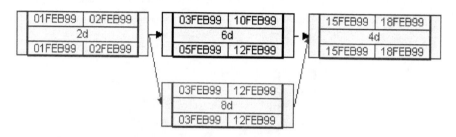

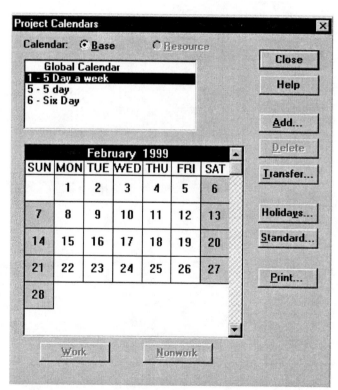

9.6 Constraints

Constraints are used to impose logic on activities that cannot be realistically scheduled with logic links. This chapter covers in detail four constraints:

- **Start constraint – Early**

- **Finish constraint – Late**

- **Expected finish** and

- **Float constraint – As late as possible**.

Early Constraints operate on the **Early Dates** and **Late Constraints** operate on **Late Dates**.

These are the minimum number of constraints that you will require to make your schedule work.

Start constraint – Early, also known as **Start no Earlier Than** constraint, is used when the start date of an activity is known or known approximately. P3 will not allow the activity's early start to be prior this date.

Finish Constraint – Late, also known as **Finish no Later** constraint, is used when the latest finish date is stipulated. P3 will not allow the activity's late finish to be after this date.

A date with a constraint will be displayed with an asterisk. Eg 03JUN00*. The asterisk for and Early Constraints will only be displayed in the Early date column and Late Constraints in the Late date column.

Expected Finish, is used to calculate the remaining duration for you. P3 will calculate the remaining duration as the number of working days left between the start date (data date if in progress) and the expected finish.

The Remaining duration of an activity assigned with an Expected Finish constraint will be displayed with an asterisk. E.g. 10*.

Float constraint – As late as possible, also known as **Zero Free Float**, is used to make the activity early finish immediately prior to its successors. A classical example is the "just in time" delivery of materials before installation.

The other constraints are:

- **Start constraint – Late**   Start no later than

- **Finish constraint – Early**   Finish no earlier than

- **Start on**   Start no earlier than and Start no later than

- **Mandatory Start/Finish**   Nominates the dates and violates the logic and

- **Float constraint**

  – Zero total float   Removes all positive float.

9.6.1   Constraints Form

To impose constraints on an activity, you should select the activity then:

- Press the right mouse button, and choose **Activity Detail**, **Constraints** from the menu or
- Use **View**, **Activity Detail** and choose **Constraints** or
- Click on the constraints toolbar icon 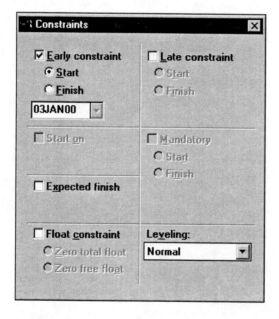.

The **Constraints** form is then displayed.

- Click on the constraint required then
- Select the Constraint date.

The **Leveling** option is discussed in the **RESOURCE LEVELLING** chapter.

9.6.2   Project Must Finish by Constraint

It is also possible to impose an absolute finish date on the project using **the Project Overview** form.

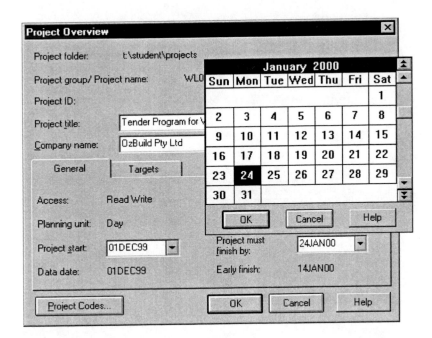

Imposing a **Project must finish by** date results in P3 calculating the late dates from this date rather than the calculated early finish date. Therefore a **Project must finish by** later than the calculated early finish date will introduce **Positive Float** to the project. A **Project must finish by** later than the calculated early finish date will introduce **Positive Float** to the project.

Float is calculated by subtracting the early date from the late date.

Positive Float is created when the early date is earlier than the late date and there is spare time to complete the activity or project.

Negative Float is created when the early date is later than the late date and there is insufficient time to complete the activity or project. Negative float may be created by imposing **Constraints** or a **Project must finish by** date.

Imposing a **Project must finish by** date may introduce **NEGATIVE** float to all activities when the calculated early finish date is later than the must finish by date but there are no activity constraints to indicate how this float has been generated.

9.7 Log Records

P3 allows you to record additional descriptions and document your planning assumptions by providing 99 records which are 48 characters in length.

The **Log** form may be displayed by:

- Selecting View, Activity Detail, Log or

- Ctrl K or

- Selecting logs in the Activity Form or

- Clicking on the Log toolbar icon 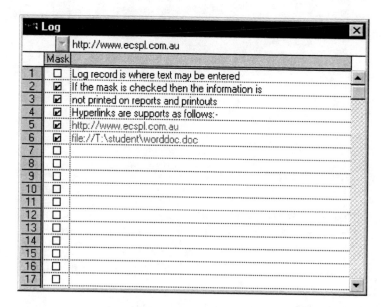 .

The log record may be used for launching other applications (see the help file for more details).

The log records may also be displayed by:

- Printing a report using the **Tools**, **Tabular Reports**, **Schedule**. (More information on Tabular Reports may be found in the Help files or manuals).

- Placing the text on bars.

Logs may not be displayed in columns.

SureTrak has a facility for accessing the first ten log records and is able to display then in columns.

WORKSHOP 12

Constraints

Preamble

Management has provided further input to your schedule.

Assignment

1. Record the calculated early finish and note the critical path of the project before applying any constraints.
2. Display the **Total Float** column
3. The client has said that they require the submission on before 24JAN00:
   a) Apply a finish no later than constraint, schedule and note dates and critical path.
   b) Apply a project must finish by constraint, schedule and note the dates and critical path.
4. Due to proximity to Christmas, management has requested that we delay the Request for Component Tenders until first thing in the New Year (03JAN00). Consensus is that a better response and sharper prices will be obtained after the Christmas rush (record this in a log record). Again measure the impact on the critical path and end dates.
5. Group the activities by Total Float and then sort by Remaining Duration (descending).
6. After review, it is agreed that one day may be trimmed from both Editing the Draft Proposal and Finalizing the Tender Package.
7. Note the change to the project end date.

10   FILTERS AND LAYOUTS

This section is designed to make you aware of the software's ability to control the presentation of information, both on the screen, and in printouts, by using **Filters** and **Layouts**.

Filters allow you to select which activities are displayed. You should use a filter when you wish to work with a small group of activities that meet a specific criteria for performing any scheduling function, such as adding logic or analyzing resources.

Once you have altered the appearance of your screen with **Organize**, **Filters** and **Format Bars** you may save your settings with the Save Layouts function and reuse them at a later date.

This chapter covers the following topics:

- Understanding how to use filters

- How to create and edit your own filters and

- How to save your own layouts.

The name of the current Layout and Filter is always displayed at the bottom of the screen in the status bar.

10.1 Understanding Filters

P3 has an ability to restrict the number of tasks displayed on the screen at any given time. You may only wish to see the Project Manager's work or perhaps Saturday work or even the work over the next couple of months. **P3** defaults to using all activities and has a number of filters already available that you might like to use, edit or delete. You may also create one or more for your own use.

Select **Format**, **Filter** or click the ▼ button on the toolbar to see the filters provided with the standard installation.

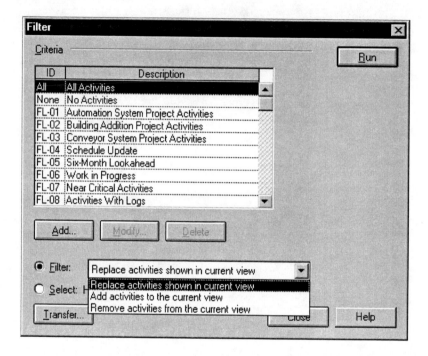

- **Transfer**, allows you to transfer filters from another project.

- **Add**, allows you to create a new filter.

- **Modify**, allows you to modify an existing filter.

- **Delete**, allows you to delete an existing filter except the **All** and **None** filter.

- The **Filter** radio button has three options in the drop down box, (shown above):
  - **Replace activities shown in current view** only displays activities that meet the filter criteria.
  - **Add activities to the current view** adds the activities that meet the filter criteria to the activities currently displayed.
  - **Remove activities from the current view** removes activities that meet the filter criteria from the activities currently displayed.

- **Select**, highlights activities that meet the filter's criteria.

10.2 Creating and Editing Filters

To demonstrate filters we will take you through the process of creating a new filter to display incomplete activities:

- Press the **Add** button to create a new filter.

- You will be presented with the **Add a New Filter** form. Enter a two character alphanumeric code that has not been used before and press the **Enter** key or click on the **OK** button.

- Enter the Description Incomplete Activities.

- From the box below Selection Criteria drop down select Percent Complete.

- In the box below Is select NE – Not Equals from the drop down box which is displayed as NE.

- In the Low Value type 100.

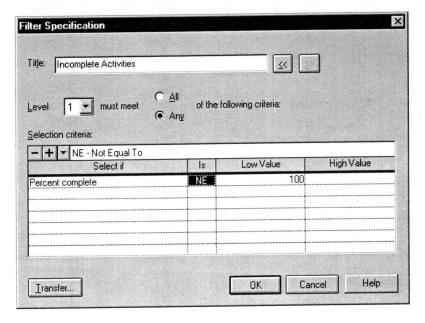

Click on **OK** and **OK** again at the **Filter Specification** form to apply this filter. Only the incomplete activities will be displayed.

- The ⬚ and ⬚ buttons display the previous and next filters in the list.

- **Transfer** allows you to transfer filters in from another project.

The Incomplete Activity filter demonstrates a simple filter showing incomplete activities.

More complex filters are possible by:

- Adding more criteria in the **Selection Criteria** combined with using the **All** and **Any** options, and/or

- Adding additional filter levels up to Level 4.

Understanding All and Any
When you add more than one selection criteria, you may use the **Any** and **All** radio buttons.

- **Any** will display activities that meet any of the criteria and

- **All** will display activities that meet all the criteria.

To display all the complete activities that are the responsibility of Angela Lowe you would create a filter shown below. The filter selects activities with Percent Complete **LT – (Less Than) 100%** and Responsibility equals **ARL – Angela Lowe**.

If **Any** is selected then all incomplete activities and all the activities that are Angela Lowe's responsibility would be displayed, which is not the intention.

Therefore **All** is selected and the displayed activities will be the Responsibility of Angela Lowe and be incomplete.

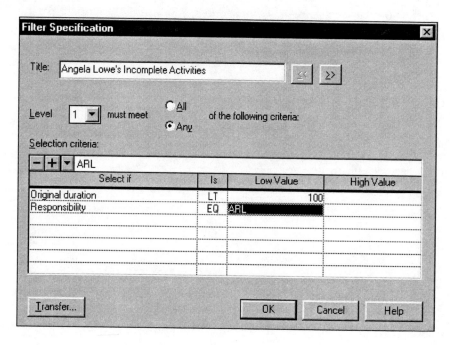

Understanding Rolling Dates

Rolling dates is a facility used in filters and other areas such as printing. For example should you wish to create a filter that selects all the activities that start within 14 days of the Data Date then you would use **Rolling Dates**.

When a date field is selected the **Low Value** and **High Value** field will allows you to select:

- **Calendar Date** and you may then select a calendar date for the criteria.

- **Start Date** to select the start date for the criteria.

- **Data Date** which is the current date of a progressed schedule. As you have not progressed our schedule the Data date is the same as the Start date. The Data date will be covered in more detail in the **TRACKING PROGRESS** chapter.

- **Finish Date** is the calculated finish date or the nominated date in the **Project must finish by** field found in **File, Project Overview**.

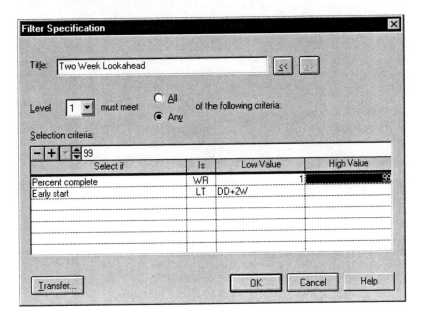

Use the drop down box to select a date and then type a displacement in hours **H**, days **D**, weeks **W**, months **M** or years **Y**.

The example above **DD+2W** selects the Data date plus 2 weeks. The **DD** is inserted by the P3 and you type in the +2W. As the project progresses, the calculated date will always be 2 weeks ahead of the Data date.

Understanding Filter Levels

- **Level 1** through to **Level 4** allows you to create more complex filters that can not be created with one level.

- Each filter level has the options of **And** and **Or**.

- At each level you may use up to five criteria for the selection of activities.

Below is an example of a filter used for showing a two-week look ahead with two Levels:

- The **Percent complete** criteria selects any activity that is not complete.

- The **Early start** selects any activity that has an Early start date less than 14 days in the future.

Level 1

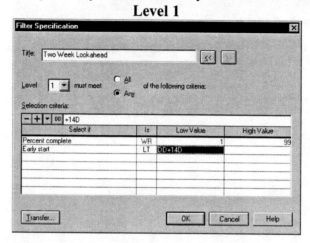

To select activities assigned to Angela Lowe or Carol Peterson you will need to go to a second level.

Level 2

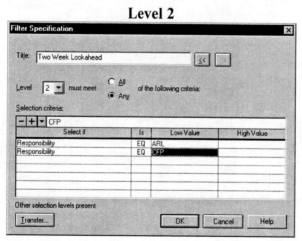

- This time you will have selected **Any** so the filter picks up both **ARL & CFP**.

- The bottom left hand side of the form has a message **Other selection levels present**. This indicates there is more than one level in the filter.

Modifying Filters

Editing filters follows the same principals as creating filters:

- In the Filter menu select the filter you wish to edit and

- Click on the **Modify** button.

Deleting Filters

A filter may be deleted by selecting the filter in the **Filter Specification** form and clicking on **Delete.**

Reapplying Filters

After you have made changes to data, you may wish to reapply filters to activities. This is achieved by selecting **Format**, **Run Filter Now** or clicking on the toolbar icon.

It is suggested that you experiment with the filters so you develop an understanding of what may be achieved with filters.

WORKSHOP 13

Filters

Preamble

Management has asked for reports on activities that fit certain specifications to suit their requirements.

Assignment

Apply the following filters to your project:

1. Group activities by Phase.
2. Add columns for Phase and Responsibility.
3. Create a filter that selects only the activities from both the Estimation and Proposal phases of the project.
4. Run this filter noting the activities selected.
5. Now add an additional criteria that selects activities that Scott Morrison or Angela Lowe are responsible for.
6. Run this filter and note the difference.

10.3 Layouts

Rather than restricting the data with filters, **Layouts** alter the presentation. The following type of information is saved with each layout:

- Column settings

- Bar formatting

- Organize settings

- Print settings and

- Colors.

Select **View**, **Layout** to open the **Layouts** menu or click on the toolbar to open an existing layout.

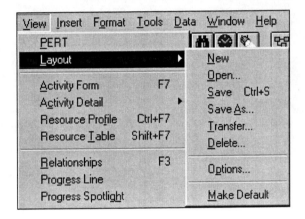

- **New** allows you to create a new layout

- **Open** is to open an existing layout

- **Save** saves a layout and is used when you have modified a layout

- **Save As** allows you to make a copy of an existing layout

- **Transfer** is to transfer layouts for another schedule

- **Delete** deletes the highlighted layout

- **Options** allows you to decide how the filter associated with a layout is applied and

- **Make Default** sets the current layout as the default layout for all new projects.

> In P3 Layouts are stored as part of the project file and are not common to all projects. In SureTrak layouts are save separately to the project files and are available to all projects. When you open a SureTrak file with P3, you will not be able to access the SureTrak Layouts and you will have to recreate them.

10.3.1 Creating a New Layout

Select **View, Layout, New**.

- When you have made changes to the current layout, you will be presented with the Save Layout form, asking you if you wish to save the changes to the current layout before you are presented with a new layout. Select Yes to save the changes you have made or No to discard changes you have made.

- You will then have a new layout that you may edit to your requirements.

- When you have made the changes to the new layout and wish to save the layout select View, Layout, Save As.

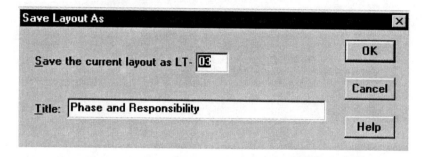

- You then type in the two-character code, should you do not wish to use the P3 nominated code, and enter the title of the filter.

10.3.2 Saving Changes to a Layout

After you have made changes to your layout you may save the changes by selecting **View, Layout, Save** or selecting another layout and you will be given the option of saving the changes to the displayed layout.

10.3.3 Layout Options

View, Layout, Options allows you to nominate how the filter that is associated with a Layout is applied.

10.3.4 Default Layout

When you create a layout that you wish to use as the default for all new schedules, select **View, Layout, Make Default**. This layout will now be displayed each time you create a new layout unless you make a copy of an existing layout with **View, Layout, Save As**.

WORKSHOP 14

Layouts

Preamble

We need a new report, which we will print as specified below.

Assignment

1. Remove your filter by selecting the ALL Activities filter.

2. Create a new layout R1 titled Workshop 14 with the following attributes

Columns

Activity ID, Arial Bold 8 centered
Description, Arial 8
Original Duration Arial 8 and
Total Float, Arial 8.

Bars

Show Early Bar only
Description Arial 8 bold, above the bar (Top)
Early Start Arial 8 left of the bar and
Early Finish Arial 8 right of the bar.

Organized

Group Responsibility Arial 10 bold, white text on blue background,
Sort on Early Start and
Total Bar at top of each group.

Timescale

Weeks.

Your screen should look like this:

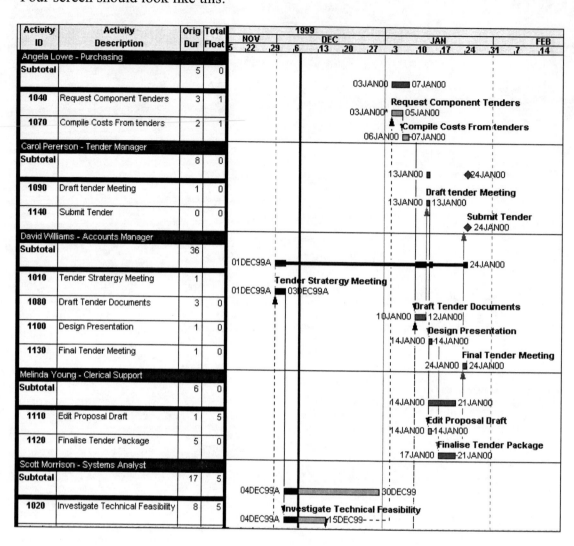

11 PRINTING AND REPORTS

P3 has many options for printing and reporting project data. P3 also has a **Tabular Reporting** (text) and a **Graphical Reporting** module in addition to the standard printing that will be covered in detail in this chapter.

This chapter will examine the following topics:

- How to create and delete page breaks

- The print preview screen and the options at print preview including setting the titles

- Page set up

- The grayscale options

- Print setup where you may also print to a file and

- Picture Preview where you may save your report in Windows metafile format.

A recommended practice is to take a complete copy of your project each time you report to the client or management to allow you to reproduce these reports at any time in the future. You may save the project into the same directory provided you change the file name.

11.1 Page Breaks

The page break option allows you to insert or remove a page break.

- Select **View**, **Page Breaks** to see the page breaks on the screen.

- You may then manually insert page breaks using **Insert**, **Page Break** or **Ctl Enter** and

- Remove all the page breaks by **Insert**, **Clear all page breaks**.

- The page breaks are displayed with a blue shade line across the screen.

11.2 Printing the Bar Chart

You are now at the stage of being able to print out the schedule. To do this use **File**, **Print Preview** or use the button on the toolbar to view the printout.

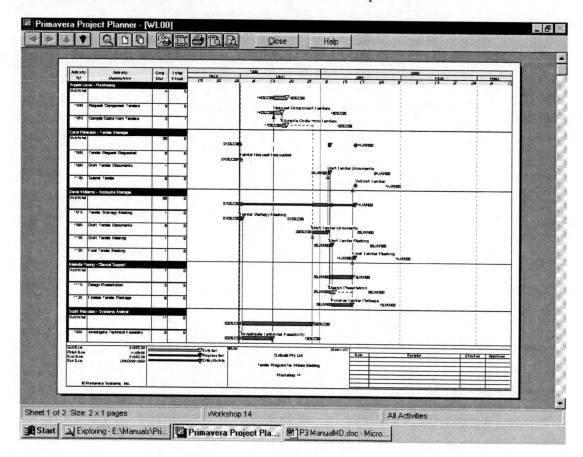

At the top of the screen there are 12 icons. From left to right the icons are:

- The 4 icons allow scrolling when a printout has more than one page.

- The is for zooming in and zooming out.

- The next two icons display one or all pages.

- The next three are for **Print set up**, **Page setup**, **Printing**.

- The **Close** icon on the left returns you to the normal view.

- The last is **Help**.

11.3 Page Setup

To open the **Page Setup** form select either:

- **File**, **Page Setup** from the normal view or

- Click on the **Page Setup** icon in the **Print Preview** screen.

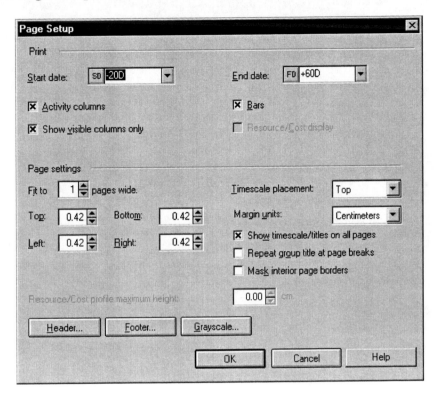

- **Start dates** and **End dates** are set as **Rolling dates** and are described in the **FILTERS AND LAYOUTS** chapter.

- The **Activity columns** box will hide the data columns when unchecked.

- **Show visible columns only** will display only whole columns visible in the normal view.

- Uncheck the **Bars** box to hide the bars.

- The **Resource/Cost Display** box will be available as an option if your layout is displaying a Resource Table or a Resource Profile. You may then decide if you wish to print the table or profile as part of your report.

- You may nominate how many pages wide using Fit to [1] pages wide. A zero entered here will let P3 calculate how many pages are needed.

- **Margin units** may be Inches, Centimeters or Points and margin sizes set in the Top, Left, Bottom and Right boxes.

- **Timescale placement** allows you to place the timescale on the top of a sheet, the bottom or both.

- Uncheck **Show timescale/titles on all pages** to place the timescale and titles only on the first page.

- **Repeat group title at page breaks** reprints the last group title from Organize above the first activity on the new page.

- Should you wish to paste a multiple page report together then **Mask interior page borders** prevents a thick line being printed around interior joins.

- Resource or Cost profiles often become distorted during printing, so the height may be controlled using the **Resource/Cost profile maximum height**.

- **Grayscale...** allows you to nominate the darkness of colors when printed in black & white. (Further detail on the next page).

- **Header...** and **Footer...** open the Header and Footer forms for formatting the Header and Footer. (Further details after Grayscale).

11.3.1 Grayscale

Grayscale is a facility for specifying how printers will print colors. You are therefore able to ensure that all colors are printed in different shades on black and white printers.

Select the color in the top half of the form, by clicking on it, and nominate the darkness it is printed by altering the **Luminosity slide control** on the lower right hand side. The bottom section shows how all the colors will be printed.

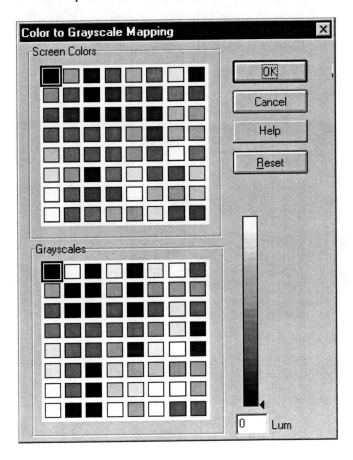

- This option will only work if the **Use Grayscale output** option is checked in the **Print Setup**.

- **Reset** sets the grayscale back to the default settings.

11.3.2 Header and Footer forms

The **Header** and **Footer** forms are the same as each other. Below is displayed the **Footer** form.

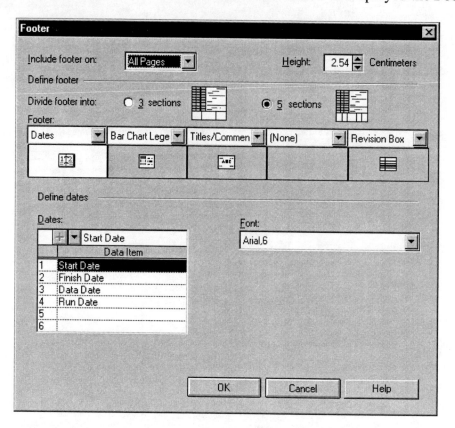

- Include footer (or header) on **first**, **last**, **all** or **no** pages sets the pages on which the footer (or header) are printed on.

- The **Height** controls the vertical size of the header or footer.

- **Divide footer into** 3 or 5 sections. Each section may be filled with one of the data types list below:
  - Selected **Dates** such as **Start**, **Data and Finish**.
  - **Titles/Comments** to identify the company and project.
  - **Logo** allows you to select a graphical file as a logo using the **Primavera Symbol Selection** form.
  - **Revision box** to indicate publishing and approval process.
  - **Bar Chart legend** to tailor the contents on the Bar Chart.

- **Font** sets the default font.

11.4 Print Set Up

To open the **Print Setup** form select either:

- **File**, **Print Setup** from the normal view or

- Click on the **Print Setup** icon in the **Print Preview** screen.

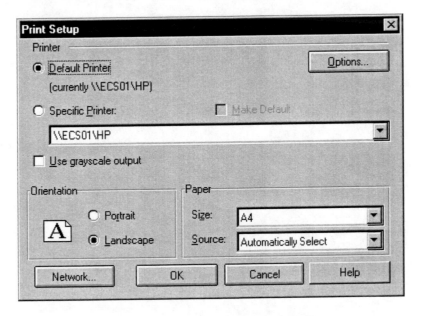

- You may select the **Default Printer** or select a **Specific Printer** from the drop down box.

- Click in **Use grayscale output** to convert the colors to a user defined grayscale.

- **Paper** allows you to select paper size and tray.

- **Options** and **Network** allow you to access the printer and network settings.

11.5 Print

To open the **Print** form select either:

- **File**, **Print** from the normal view or

- Click on the **Print** icon in the **Print Preview** screen.

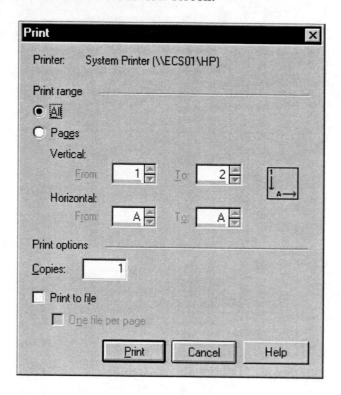

- Horizontal pages are numbered with letters starting at A for the left-hand side column.

- You may select one file for all pages or one file per page when printing to a file.

11.6 Preview Picture

Preview picture allows you to save your printout in Windows metafile format, which has a **.wmf** extension. Your reports may then be simply inserted into other documents that accept this format of graphics. Select **File, Preview Picture**:

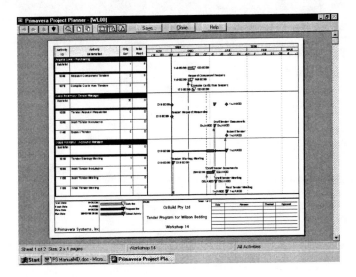

- All the options are the same as printing.

- Select **Save** to save the file.

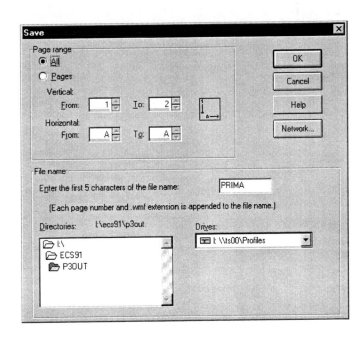

- Nominate the pages to be saved as files,

- Nominate the drive and directory in which to save the files,

- Nominate a five-character name for the files. The files are saved with this name and the consecutive numbers from 001 onwards for each sheet.

11.7 Save as Web Page

P3 has a good facility for creating a web page. Select **File, Save as Web Page** to open the **Save as Web Page** form.

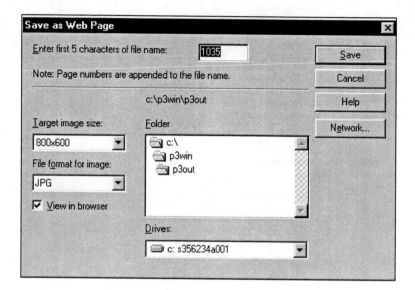

- Enter a five character name for the web page.

- Nominate the **Target image size** and **File format for image**, JPG or PNG.

- Select the drive and folder.

- P3 will create a web page and a graphical file for each for each page of the report. The reports are all linked so you my move easily from one page to the next.

11.8 Reports

P3 has two reporting facilities:

- **Tabular Reports** which are accessed using **Tools, Tabular Reports** and

- **Graphical Reports** which are accessed using **Tools, Graphical Reports**.

These reporting functions are not covered in this book.

WORKSHOP 15

Reports

Preamble

After we issued our R1-Workshop 14 report, we received a request to further tailor it.

Assignment

1. Modify this layout to have:
   - Set Start date to be Start date –10 days.
   - Set Finish date to be Finish date +20 days.
   - Show all columns and bars.
   - Make all margins 1 cm.
   - Show timescale on every page.
   - Repeat group titles at each page break.
   - Set the Title font to be Arial 12 Bold
   - Center Title 1 – Tender Program for Wilson Bedding.
   - Center Title 2 – OzBuild Pty Ltd.
   - Show revision box.
   - Logo – place any logo next to the revision box.

2. Close your print preview and save your layout as R2, title Workshop 15.

Your print preview screen should look like this:

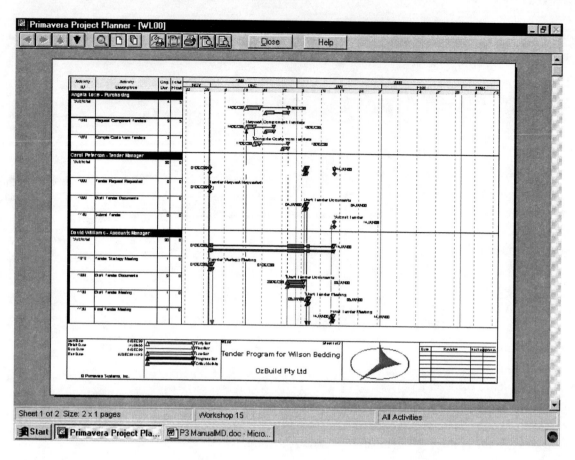

12 TRACKING PROGRESS

You have now completed the plan or have completed sufficient iterations to have an acceptable plan and the project is progressing. The important phase of regular monitoring begins. Monitoring is important to help catch problems as early as possible, and thus to help minimize the impact of the problem on the successful completion of the project.

P3 uses an entire schedule as the target. Therefore the schedule is copied into the same subdirectory with a different name, before a project is statused for the first time. It is then selected as the Target.

To monitor progress, the actual progress is recorded and entered into the schedule and the schedule is calculated. This process is known as statusing, progressing or updating a schedule. The progressed schedule is compared to the Target to identify where the project is behind or ahead of plan.

Two target schedules may be linked to the project you are working on at any time. This is useful for comparing the current schedule with the target and the last period schedule at the same time, thus enabling you to see the variance from the target and last periods in the same View. The target schedules may be changed at any time.

The main steps for monitoring progress are:

- copying an unprogressed schedule as the Target Schedule
- assigning the Target project(s) to the schedule
- recording or Marking up progress
- updating the schedule
- calculating the schedule and
- comparing and reporting actual progress against planned progress and revising the schedule if required.

This chapter will explain these steps.

12.1 Copying a Schedule

The P3 schedule is made up of a number of files. To ensure all files are copied it is recommended to use the **Copy** function to copy schedules. Select **Tools**, **Project Utilities**, **Copy** to open the **Copy** form below:

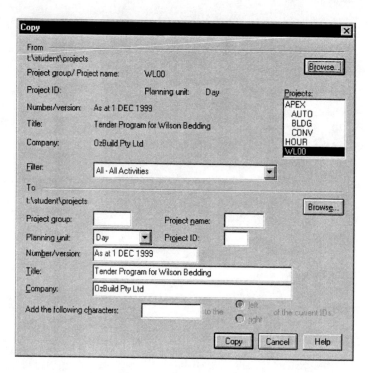

In the **From** area of the **Copy** form:

- Select the folder that you wish to copy from using **Browse**.

- Select the Project or Project Group you wish to copy under Projects and

- When you only require to copy some activities then select a filter.

In the **To** area of the **Copy** form:

- When you are copying a project that is not part of a Project Group, fill in only the project name in Project Group as above.

- **Planning unit** allows you to change the planning unit when you copy a project but you will have to change the durations using **Global Change** after the copy, as calendars are altered but not durations.

- **Number/version**, **Title** and **Company** may be edited.

- **Browse** allows you to copy to another folder. If you wish the project to become a target, it must be copied into the same directory.

- **Add the following characters** allows you to add additional characters to the left or right of the Activity ID's of the newly created project.

- **Project name** and **Project ID** are completed when copying between Projects or Project Group and Project.

12.2 Setting the Target

To set the target select **Tools**, **Project Utilities**, **Target** to open the **Targets** form:

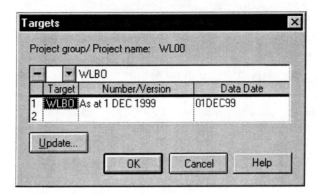

- From the dropdown box select the projects you wish to be Target 1 and Target 2.

- **Update** is a facility for updating the target with information from the current schedule.

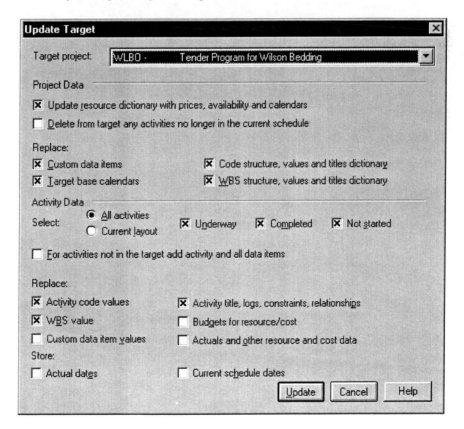

12.3 Recording Progress

Normally a project has a nominated status date that could be typically once a week or once a month. Progress is recorded on the status date and the scheduler updates the schedule when the information is received.

It is best to concentrate on the remaining duration of any activity, and not the percentage complete when statusing an activity. The **Remaining Duration** is the duration from the Data Date to the Earliest Finish of the Activity. This is because the durations are estimated in the first place and, as it progresses, you get a better idea of how long the task actually still has to go. Typical information to be recorded is:

- When the activity started

- The Remaining Duration or when it is expected to finish

- The percentage complete and

- The finish date of completed activities.

A markup is often done in pen on a copy of the current schedule and is best done by a physical inspection of the work, although that is not always possible. It is good practice to keep this record for your own reference at later date. Ensure that you mark the date of the markup (ie the data date) and if relevant, the time.

A markup sheet may be printed from P3 by creating a layout with the appropriate columns including a filter that displays only in progress activities or will start in the next two periods. It would also have sufficient space for people to write update information on the printout.

P3 also has an email facility that may be used for gathering status information.

It is best to calculate the percent complete from a predefined set of parameters. People are usually optimistic about their progress when it is guessed. If the % complete is difficult to determine for some activities, such as writing a specification, then it is suggested that an agreed set of status points are used with an agreed % complete for each point. For example:

- 10% for starting the document

- 50% for first draft

- 80% for submission for approval and

- 1005 for an approved document.

12.4 Updating or Statusing the Schedule

The next stage is to update the schedule by entering the markup information into the schedule and rescheduling to determine the net effect.

The activity form may be used for statusing activities.

Activity in Progress

For an activity in progress, you should enter the following information:

- Set the **Actual Start** date by clicking on **AS** and selecting correct date from the dropdown box or typing in the date.

- Enter the **Percent Complete** in the **Pct** box.

- Enter the **Remaining Duration** in the **RD** box.

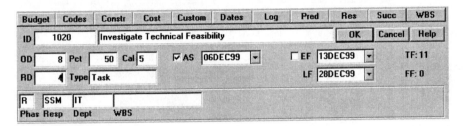

Completed Activity

For a complete activity, you should enter the following information:

- Set the **Actual Start** date by clicking on **AS** and selecting correct date from the dropdown box or typing in the date.

- Set the **Actual Finish** date by clicking on **AF** and selecting the correct date from the dropdown box or typing in the date.

- P3 will set the Percent Complete to 100 for any activity that is assigned an **Actual Finish**.

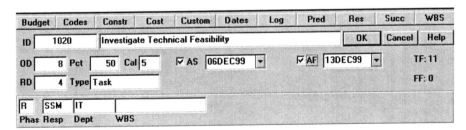

12.5 Suspend and Resume

When you wish to Suspend the work and Resume an activity at a later date. Open the **Date** form from the **Activity Form** or by clicking on the Dates button in the **Task** form, and enter the Suspend and Resume dates.

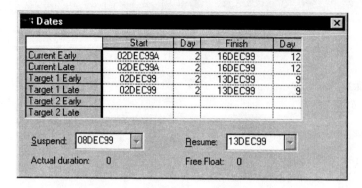

The example above shows an activity suspended from 8 Dec 99 to the 13 Dec 99.

Normally the Suspend date is in the past and the Resume date in the future.

12.6 Linking Remaining Duration and Schedule Percent Complete

Before you calculate the schedule, you should be aware of some parameters. P3 has a facility of **Linking remaining duration and schedule percent complete**. Therefore when you enter a Percent Complete the Remaining Duration is calculated for you and if you enter the Remaining Duration, the Percent Complete is calculated for you. This is often not realistic and therefore it is recommended to unlink these.

Select **Tools**, **Options**, **Autocost Rules** and uncheck the **Linking remaining duration and schedule percent complete** box. You will now be able to enter the Percent Complete and Remaining Duration independently.

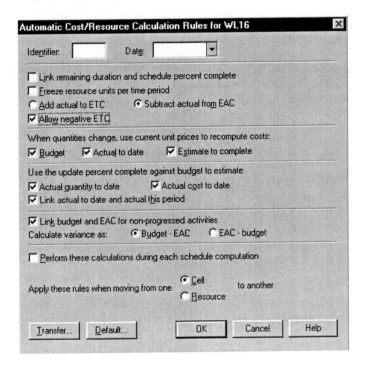

12.7 Calculating the Schedule

Now you may reschedule by selecting **Tools**, **Schedule**

- Select the new data date.

- Click on **OK**.

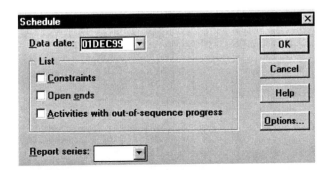

WORKSHOP 16

Updating progress

Preamble

You are at the end of the first week and need to update the progress and reforecast.

Assignment

1. Create a Target Project with the name WLB0 by copying your current schedule and setting this as your Target 1.
2. Ensure that the percentage complete and remaining duration are unlinked in your Autocost rules.
3. Status the project using all the methods described and from the data below:

Activity ID	Activity Description	Orig Dur	Rem Dur	% Comp	Early Start	Early Finish
1000	Tender Request Requested	0	0	100	01DEC99A	
1010	Tender Stratergy Meeting	1	0	100	01DEC99A	03DEC99A
1020	Investigate Technical Feasibility	8	6	90	04DEC99A	15DEC99
1030	Document Installation	4	4	0	16DEC99	20DEC99
1040	Request Component Tenders	3	3	0	03JAN00*	05JAN00
1050	Develop Project Schedule	4	4	0	21DEC99	24DEC99
1060	Draft Technical Details	9	9	0	16DEC99	30DEC99
1070	Compile Costs From tenders	2	2	0	06JAN00	07JAN00
1080	Draft Tender Documents	3	3	0	10JAN00	12JAN00
1090	Draft tender Meeting	1	1	0	13JAN00	13JAN00
1100	Design Presentation	1	1	0	14JAN00	14JAN00
1110	Edit Proposal Draft	1	1	0	14JAN00	14JAN00
1120	Finalise Tender Package	5	5	0	17JAN00	21JAN00
1130	Final Tender Meeting	1	1	0	24JAN00	24JAN00
1140	Submit Tender	0	0	0		24JAN00

4. Re-schedule as at 08DEC99.
5. Reformat your columns to reflect the layout above:
   - Sort Activities by Activity ID
   - Remove text from bars
   - Display progress on bars based on % complete and
   - Change timescale settings and sightlines.
6. Save the Layout as S1 - Statusing Layout.

12.8 Comparison

There will have been some changes to the schedule. The full extent of the change is not apparent without having a Target with which to compare with. To show the **Target Bar** in the **Bar Chart** select **Format, Bars**:

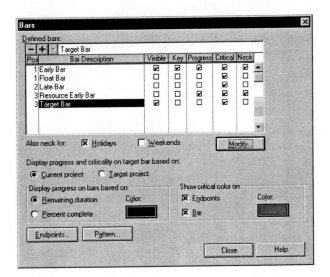

- Add a new bar by clicking on the [+] to open the **Add Bar Definition** form.

- Enter **Target Bar** as description.

- Select Start point as Target 1 early start.

- Select End point as Target 1 early finish.

- Change the color and end point if you wish.

- Set the **Position** as 3 to put the Target bar below the current schedule.

- Select **OK** and you will be returned to the **Bars** form.

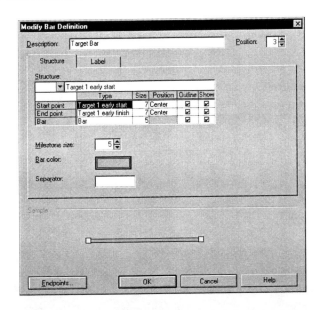

12.9 Corrective Action

There are two courses of action available with slippage. The first is to accept the slippage. Though this is rarely acceptable, but it is the easy answer. Secondly is to look and see if you could improve the new end date by reducing durations or changing relationships.

When you find possible solutions to return the project to its original completion date, you must confirm the changes with the person responsible for the project as this will obviously impact on the work.

WORKSHOP 17

Baseline Comparison

Preamble

You are at the end of the first week, have updated the schedule and need to report progress/slippage.

Assignment

1. Format your bars and columns to reflect the view below:
   - Create a target bar, and remove critical color on endpoints and bar.
   - Place the bar in position 2.
   - Create the extra column Variance 1 Early Finish.

Activity ID	Activity Description	Orig Dur	Rem Dur	%	Early Start	Early Finish	Variance 1 Early Finish
100	Tender Request Requested	0	0	100	01DEC99A		0
101	Tender Strategy Meeting	1	0	100	01DEC99A	03DEC99A	-3
102	Investigate Technical	8	6	90	04DEC99A	15DEC99	-3
106	Draft Technical Details	9	9	0	16DEC99	30DEC99	-3
103	Document Installation	4	4	0	16DEC99	20DEC99	-4
105	Develop Project Schedule	4	4	0	21DEC99	24DEC99	-4
104	Request Component Tenders	3	3	0	03JAN00*	05JAN00	0
107	Compile Costs From tenders	2	2	0	06JAN00	07JAN00	0
108	Draft Tender Documents	3	3	0	10JAN00	12JAN00	0
109	Draft tender Meeting	1	1	0	13JAN00	13JAN00	0
110	Design Presentation	1	1	0	14JAN00	14JAN00	0
111	Edit Proposal Draft	1	1	0	14JAN00	14JAN00	0
112	Finalise Tender Package	5	5	0	17JAN00	21JAN00	0
113	Final Tender Meeting	1	1	0	24JAN00	24JAN00	0
114	Submit Tender	0	0	0		24JAN00	0

2. The report shows where the project activities have fallen behind schedule and by how many days.

13 SCHEDULING OPTIONS AND OUT OF SEQUENCE PROGRESS

Scheduling Options allow you to decide how P3 calculates and displays the following date and duration information:

- Automatic scheduling and Leveling

- Out of sequence progress

- Start to Start Lag

- Activity Durations with Finish to Finish relationships

- Open Ends, activities without successors

- Total Float Calculations for Interruptible Scheduling and Hammocks

Select **Tools**, **Schedule**, **Options** to open the **Scheduling/Level Calculations Options** form:

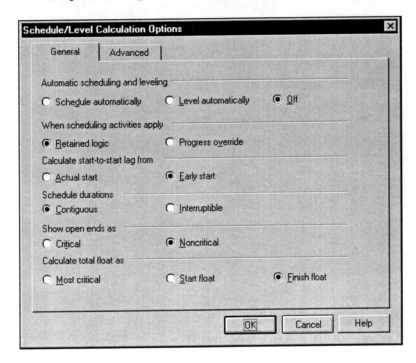

13.1 Automatic Scheduling and Leveling

P3 has an Automatic Scheduling and Leveling Option. The project will be scheduled and/or leveled as appropriate when data is changed.

Select **Tools**, **Schedule**, **Options** icon to open the **Schedule/Level Calculations Options** form:

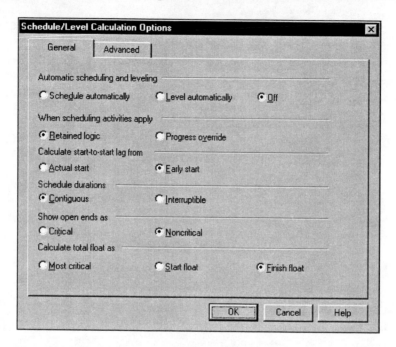

- Select **Off** and P3 will only schedule when you press **F9**, select **Tools**, **Schedule**, **Schedule Now** or click on the ⊕ icon on the Tool Bar.

- Select **Schedule automatically** and P3 will schedule each time data that affects that timing, such as durations, constraints and logic, is changed.

- Select **Level automatically** and P3 will level the schedule each time you make changes to resources and recalculate the schedule.

13.2 Out-of-Sequence Progress

Out of Sequence Progress decides how original logic applies to the remaining work of a partially completed activity with an incomplete predecessor.

There are two options for calculating this relationship in P3:

- Retained Logic and

- Progress Override.

Retained Logic

The diagram below shows the effect of selecting **Retained logic**. The remaining work on the activity is scheduled to be completed after the predecessor.

Activity ID	Activity Description	Orig Dur	Rem Dur	%	1999 JUN
1000	First Activity	10	5	50	
1020	Second Activity	10	9	10	

Progress Override

Below shows the effect of **Progress override** where any remaining work continues uninterrupted and ignores the predecessor logic.

Activity ID	Activity Description	Orig Dur	Rem Dur	%	1999 JUN
1000	First Activity	10	5	50	
1020	Second Activity	10	9	10	

This option affects all in progress activities and you will have to decide which is the most appropriate for your project.

13.3 Start-to-Start Lag.

When a Predecessor has started, P3 may calculate the Start-to-Start Lag based on the Actual Start or the calculated Early Start. The calculations to determine this lag are complex, see the **Help menu** should you wish to have an understanding of how P3 calculates the Lag.

It is suggested that you base your lag on the Actual Start date.

13.4 Activity Durations with Finish-to-Finish relationships

When an activity has a Finish-to-Finish relationship then the finish date of the successor activity is determined by the predecessor.

The Start date may be calculated in two ways:

- Subtracting the activity duration from the finish date to calculate the start date. When this calculation is used, the activity duration is described as **Contiguous**.

- Calculating the schedule start date from the activity predecessor start date and the end date from the Finish-to-Finish relationship. Thus the total duration of the activity may be greater than the assigned duration and then the activity duration is described as **Interruptible**.

You should then set the **Schedule durations** as according to how you want your durations calculated. It is suggested that you choose **Contiguous** under normal circumstances so that the displayed duration will be the same as the assigned duration.

13.5 Open Ends

An open end is created by an activity without a successor. Therefore, you may show open end activities as critical or not critical.

It is recommended that you should ensure that all activities have a predecessor and successor and therefore creating a closed network except the start and finish milestones.

When you have open ended activities it is suggested that they are displayed as critical as a reminder that they are a potential problem.

13.6 Total Float Calculations for Interruptible Scheduling and Hammocks

Float may be calculated by subtracting:

- Early Start from Late Start or

- Early Finish from Late Finish.

Therefore, there would be different float durations for activities with:

- Interruptible Start dates and

- Hammock activities.

It is suggested that you use **Most Critical** as default as this will display the least float.

WORKSHOP 18

Out of Sequence

Assignment

1. Create a new project called SSLG.
   - Project start date 7 Jun 99
   - Planning Unit of Days
   - Work Days per week of 5 days
2. Add two activities of 10 days duration as detailed in the paragraph Out of Sequence Progress.
3. Chain Link the two activities.
4. Reschedule with a data date of 7 Jun 99.
5. Update to reflect the out-of -sequence condition shown in this chapter.
6. Recalculate the schedule with the settings under **Tools**, **Schedule**, **Options** set to:
   - Retained logic, and then
   - Progress override
   - Close the project

14 ACTIVITY ID'S, WBS CODES AND ALIAS

Activity Codes were discussed earlier as a method of organizing activities under project breakdown structures. There are two alternative tools available in P3 for organizing activities in a schedule:

- Activity ID Codes and
- WBS Codes.

Alias is a facility for merging the activities from two codes under one heading which may be used for **Tabular Reports** and **Graphical Reports**.

There is another method of organizing activities used by some software called **Outlining**. Outlining is used by MS Project and SureTrak but is not available in P3.

When a SureTrak project with Outlining or a Microsoft Project file is imported into P3, the **Topic** activities which are created by Microsoft Project may not be "Promoted" or "Demoted" in P3 but they may be deleted. It is recommended that they are deleted.

14.1 Activity ID Codes

The **Activity ID Code** is assigned to an activity as part of the Activity ID and therefore puts logic into the Activity ID.

Activities assigned with Activity ID Codes are organized in **Layouts** in the same method as activities assigned with Activity Codes. You have the option of choosing either **Activity Codes** or **Activity IDs** when creating a Layout.

In the example below, an Activity ID Code has been assigned for the Subproject, the Phases and the Disciplines. The values are seen in the first four characters in the Activity ID.

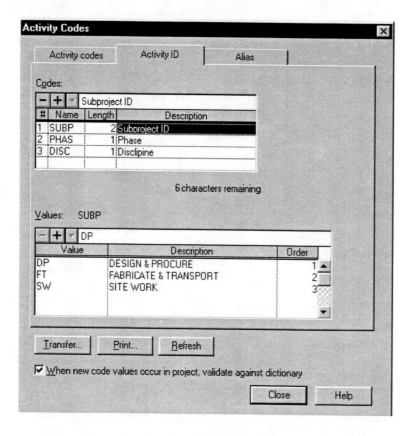

SUBP is a special Activity ID Code which is used by P3 to identify Activities belonging to a Project within a Project Group.

Defining Activity IDs

Select, **Data**, **Activity Codes** and the **Activity Code** option button.

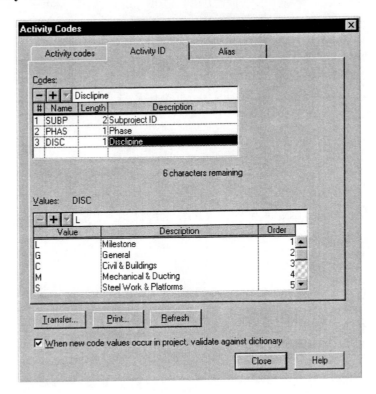

- Use ▣ to create a new Activity ID Code.

- **Length** will indicate the number of characters in the Activity ID Code.

- **Value** and **Order** are entered in the same way as Activity Codes.

- The **Value** is typed in as part of the Activity ID.

- **Transfer** allows importing of codes from another project.

When more than one Activity ID Code is created, then the first code defines the leftmost characters in the Activity ID. The second ID Code defines the next characters in the Activity ID, and so on.

Activity ID Codes are selected and used in **Layouts** in the same way as Activity Codes. Activity Codes and Activity ID Codes may be mixed in the same layout.

Disadvantage of Activity ID Codes

Complex use of Activity ID Codes may make it difficult to add new activities. You will have to type in the correct codes in the Activity ID when adding an activity.

Advantages of Activity ID Codes

Well planned Activity ID's make it easy to find activities and add logic in large projects. This is because when you type the first character of an Activity ID in an Activity ID drop down box the software takes you to the correct place in the list of activities.

It is suggested that you consider using

- **Activity ID Codes** for activity attributes that are unlikely to change such as Phase or Discipline and

- **Activity Codes** for attributes that may change such as Responsibility or Contractor

14.2 WBS – Work Breakdown Structure

A WBS represents a hierarchical breakdown of a project into elements. A WBS may be used to represent any of the following:

- WBS   Work Breakdown Structure, which breaks down the project into the Work required to complete a project.

- OBS   Organisation Breakdown Structure, showing the hierarchical structure of a project.

- CBS   Contract Breakdown Structure, showing a breakdown of contracts and subcontracts.

- SBS   System Breakdown Structure, showing the elements of a complex system.

P3 allows one hierarchical WBS structure and therefore only one of the above structures may be defined with the P3 WBS facility.

It is recommended that you use Activity Codes for all your Project Breakdown Structures unless you have specific requirements for a hierarchical WBS.

The P3 Work Breakdown Structure is a hierarchical structure to which activities are attached.

- Costs, durations and logic may not be applied to WBS codes; they are purely a structure to attach activities.

- Costs, resources and durations may be summarized at WBS levels in the same manner as organizing with Activity Codes.

- A maximum of 20 levels are available.

Creating a WBS Structure

To use the WBS facility the following steps should be followed:

- Set up the WBS Levels,

- Build the WBS Code Dictionary and

- Assign the Code to activities.

Set up the WBS Levels

- Select Define, WBS Codes, Structure

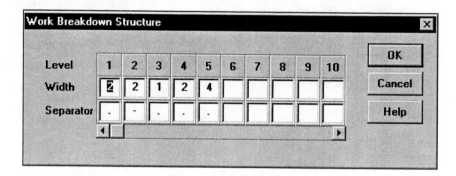

- **Width** is the number of characters you nominate per WBS level.

- **Separator** is the character that is displayed between the level codes.

- Select **OK**.

Be careful, should you wish to redefine the code width after defining and assigning WBS Codes. It is likely that the codes will end up meaningless.

Building the WBS Code Dictionary
You will now be at the WBS Codes Form.

- The code is typed in the WBS column, do not type in the separators and

- The title is typed in the **Title** column.

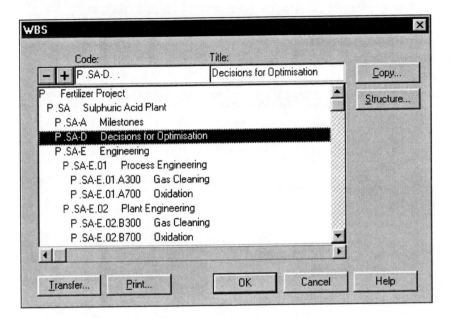

- **Transfer** allows the copying of a WBS from another project.

- **Copy** is used to copy and rename a branch of a WBS.

Assign the Code to activities
WBS codes are assigned to activities by:

- Using the WBS code box in the Activity Form,

- Displaying the WBS column or

- Dragging activities into the correct area when the project is organized by a WBS Layout.

14.3 Alias

Alias is a facility for merging the activities from two codes under one heading which may be used for **Tabular Reports** and **Graphical Reports**.

Select **Data**, **Activity Codes**, select the **Alias** tab and click on **Aliases**:

- Define your Alias, the example below shows an Alias merging Phase & responsibility.
- Click on OK.

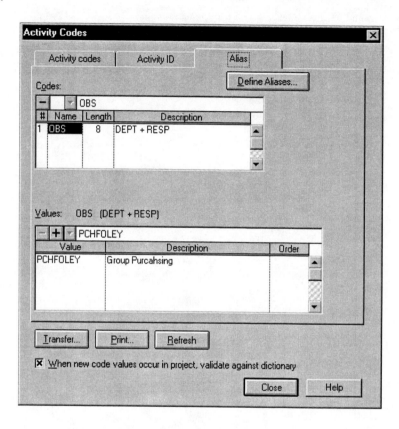

- This will return you to the **Activity Codes Dictionary** form.

At the **Activity** form:

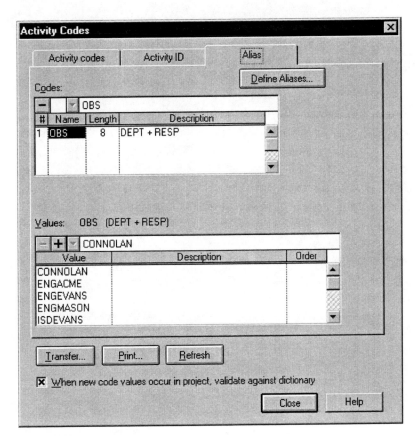

- Click on **Refresh** and P3 will fill in the **Value** column.

- You the will need to complete the **Description** and **Order**.

- Aliases may **NOT** be selected in Organize.

15 CREATING AND USING RESOURCES

A resource may be defined as something or someone that is assigned to an activity and is required to complete the task. This includes people or groups of people, materials, plant, access and money.

It is recommended that you create and assign the minimum number of resources to activities. Avoid cluttering the schedule with resources that are in plentiful supply or are of little importance.

The following steps are followed to create and use resources in a P3 schedule:

- Create your resources in the Resource Dictionary.

- Assign the resources to activities.

- Manipulate the resource calendar if resources have special timing requirements.

This chapter will cover these steps for creating and assigning resources to activities.

Before we start we will define some terminology:

- **Driving Resource**. When a Driving Resource is assigned to an activity it will determine the duration of an activity and over ride the duration entered in the **Task** form. When there is more than one Driving Resource then the Duration of the longest resource will determine the length of the Activity.

- **Non-driving Resource**. When a Non-driving Resource is assigned to an activity, it has no effect on the duration entered in the **Task** form.

 Driving Resources add an extra level of complexity to the schedule that is often not required. It is therefore recommended that all resources are entered as Non-driving unless scheduling requirements dictate that Driving resources are required.

15.1 Creating Resources

Select **Data**, **Resources** to add resources to the Resource Dictionary.

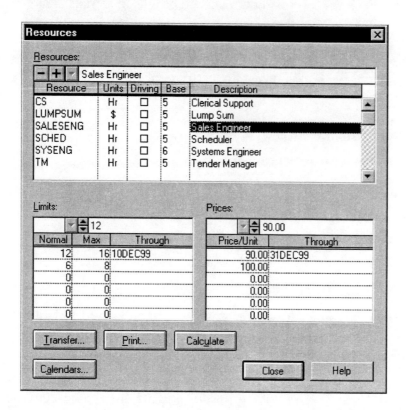

- Use the ⊞ button to insert a new resource.

- Enter the **Resource** code, (up to 8 characters long).

- Enter the **Units**, e.g. Hrs, Days, (up to 4 characters).

- **Driving**, when box is checked resources are assigned to activities as Driving. They may be changed to Non-driving after assignment to an activity. The reverse applies when the box is checked.

- **Base** is the calendar used as the default for the resource. The resource calendar stays the same as the Base calendar until it is modified.

- Enter the **Description**, (up to 40 characters).

SureTrak has a **Revenue** component which is not available in P3.

- **Normal, Max** and **Through**.
  - **Normal** is the normal number of resources you have available for a task. A zero would indicate an unlimited availability.
  - **Max** is a value intended to represent the absolute maximum number of resource units you have available. This level of availability may be indicated on histograms and used in leveling resources.
  - **Through** is the date up to which the nominated number of resources (on the same line in the Resource Dictionary) is available. The next line nominates the number of resources available between the date on the previous line and date on the next line. When there is no date on the last line then the availability is set at that level to the end of the project. The picture on the previous page shows there is a Normal Limit of 12 Sales Engineers up to 10 December 1999 and 6 thereafter.

- Enter the cost per unit in the **Price/Unit** column should you wish to calculate the cost and/or monitor cost of the resource. The **Through** date works in the same way as with availability. The previous example above shows the cost of the Sales Engineer increasing from $90.00 to $100.00 per hour on 1 Dec 99.

- **Transfer** allows transferring Resources from another project.

- **Calculate** recalculates cost based on changes made to the resources.

- **Print** prints the calendars.

- **Calendars** allow defining Resource Calendars for individual resources. This is used for defining individual holidays, etc.

    Close Out is part of a function in P3 Version 2.0 used for entering and updating costs per period. This function has been replaced by Store Period Performance in P3 Version 3.0

15.2 Hierarchical Resources

Hierarchical Resources enable you to create and work with a group of resources. The example below shows a group of design resources comprised of engineers and draftsmen grouped under a hierarchical resource **D***.

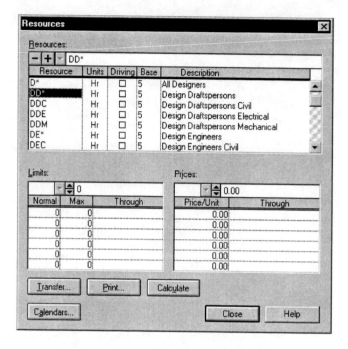

Hierarchical Resources may be used for the following purposes:

- To display the total number of resources within a Resource Group on the screen and in reports and printouts.

- You may wish to assign a **Hierarchical** resource when you are

- establishing your schedule and then at a later date substitute the Hierarchical Resource with a more specific resource from within the group.

- Hierarchical Resources may be used for Leveling.

Nominating limits in Hierarchical Resources.

- Where no limit is set on a Hierarchical resource, then the limit is calculated as the sum of all the limits of the resources in the group.

- When you set a limit for a Hierarchical resource, then the limit of the Resource Group is calculated by adding the Hierarchical Resource limit to the other resources in the group to give the total availability.

- When both a resource in the Resource Group and the Hierarchical Resource do not have a limit set, then P3 will assume unlimited resources availability for the Hierarchical Resource.

WORKSHOP 19

Defining Resources

Preamble

As we have statused our project, we need to revert to an unprogressed schedule. To achieve this we will copy the Target Schedule as our Current Schedule. The resources must now be added to this schedule.

Assignment

1. Copy WLB0 as WL01 so we have an unprogressed schedule to work with.

2. Open WL01.

3. Add the following resources to the new project by defining them in the resource dictionary:

Resource	Units	Driving	Base	Description	Price/Unit	Norm	Max	Through
CS	Hr	No	5	Clerical Support	20.00	16	24	
LUMPSUM	$	No	5	Lump Sum	0.00	0	0	
SALESENG	Hr	No	5	Sales Engineer	90.00 100.00	12 6	16 8	10DEC99
SCHED	Hr	No	5	Scheduler	60.00	8	12	
SYSENG	Hr	No	6	Systems Engineer	80.00	16	36	
TM	Hr	No	5	Tender Manager	125.00	8	8	

15.3 Assigning Resources to Activities

When a resource is assigned to an activity it has two principal components:

- The **Quantity** component of the resource which may be viewed in the **Resource** Form and

- The **Cost** component which may be viewed in the **Cost** form.

Each component has its own form. The example below shows both the **Cost** form and the **Resources** form.

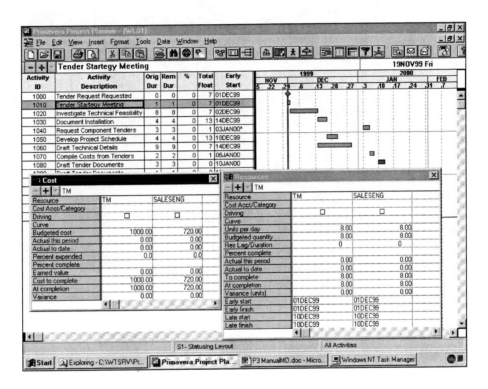

When a resource is assigned to an activity the resource data may be displayed in both **Resource** and **Cost** forms. Quantities or Costs may be zero when they are not required to be assigned a value.

The **Budget Quantity** and Budget Cost are set to equal the At Completion when a Resource is first assigned to an activity.

Resources may be assigned to activities using one of the following methods:

- Insert Resource Assignment form.

- Resource form.

- Costs form.

Assigning Resources Using Insert Resource Assignment Form
Select **Insert, Resource Assignment** or click the 🔳 button on the toolbar.

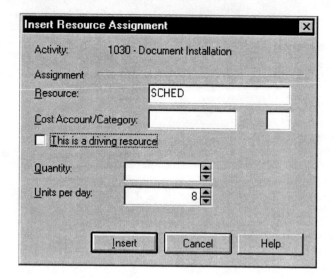

- Highlight the activity to which you wish to assign a resource.

- Select the **Resource** from the drop down box.

- Optionally assign a **Cost Account/Category.** This facility will be covered in the **TOOLS & TECHNIQUES FOR SCHEDULING** chapter.

- Check the **This is a driving resource** box if this resource is to determine the activity duration.

- Then assign the resource quantities then:
  Either
  – Click on **Quantity** and enter the total estimated quantity for this resource assignment,
  Or
  – Click on the **Units per day** (Planning Unit) and enter the number of resource units (hours, m3, crane lifts) that you expect to apply each planning unit.

- Click on **Insert** to assign another resource to an activity.

You will find you will have to experiment with this option so that you may be sure it is giving you the result you expect.

15.3.1 Assigning Resources Using Resource Form

Select **View**, **Activity Detail**, **Resources** or **Ctrl R** or select the [Res] icon in the **Activity Form**.

Resources		☒
— + ▾ SCHED		
Resource	SCHED	
Cost Acct/Category		
Driving	☐	
Curve		
Units per day	8.00	
Budgeted quantity	32.00	
Res Lag/Duration	0	
Percent complete		
Actual this period	0.00	
Actual to date	0.00	
To complete	32.00	
At completion	32.00	
Variance (units)	0.00	
Early start	14DEC99	
Early finish	17DEC99	
Late start	30DEC99	
Late finish	04JAN00	

- Click into a **Resource** and select a resource from the drop down box at the top.

- **Cost Acct/Category** may be assigned at this point. This facility will be covered in the **TOOLS & TECHNIQUES FOR SCHEDULING** chapter.

- **Driving** the default will be copied from the Resource Dictionary on assignment. It may be changed on assignment or at any time, check the box for **Driving** and uncheck for **Non-driving**.

- **Curve** is an option for assigning a **Resource/Cost Distribution** curve to the resource assignment that results in a non-linear distribution of the resource over time. This topic will be covered in the **TOOLS AND TECHNIQUES FOR SCHEDULING** chapter.

- **Units per day** is the quantity of work per time period.

- **Budget quantity** equals **Duration** x **Units per day**. The **Budget quantity** is set to equal **To complete** when a Resource is assigned.

- **Resource Lag** and **Resource Duration** are used to define the resources relationship to the duration of the activity. You specify how long after the start of the activity the resource starts work in **Lag** and for how long it will work in **Duration**.
  - When a resource is defined as **Driving** then this will calculate the duration of the Activity and supersede the duration in the **Task** form.
  - When a resource is defined as **Non-driving,** this function should be used with care as the resource may be scheduled outside the activity duration.

The remainder of the fields are used when the resource is statused and actual quantities are entered.

- **Percent Complete** is the percent of the Budget quantity used and is calculated when Actual to date quantity is entered.

- **Actual this period** is used for entering period resource usage. The calculation of this field will be covered in the **STATUSING PROJECTS WITH RESOURCES** chapter.

- **Actual to date** is the quantity consumed to date.

- **To complete** is the estimate of the quantity required to complete the task. When a resource is assigned this is the important quantity as it is the estimate to complete.

- **At completion** is the sum of **Actual to date** plus **To complete**.

- Entering **At completion** will calculate **To complete** and entering **To complete** will calculate **At completion**.

- **Variance (Units)** is **Budget** minus **At completion**.

- **Costs** are calculated using the rates in the Resource dictionary.

- The dates refer to the resource dates.

15.3.2 Assigning Resources Using Costs Form

When there are no hours or quantities associated with the activity then the **Costs** form may be used for assigning resources to activities.

Select **View**, **Activity Detail**, **Costs** or **Ctrl T** or select the [Cost] icon in the **Activity Form** to open the **Cost** form:

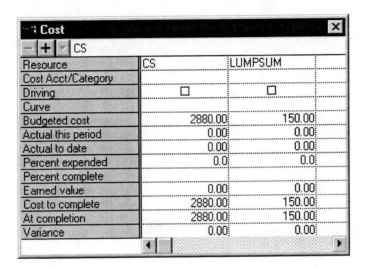

- Resources may be assigned from this box if required, and it is usually used for assigning resources that do not have quantities, such as lump sum costs.

The following fields are used when the schedule is statused and actual costs entered.

- Percent expended is proportion of Budget Spent, when Actual to date is entered.

- At completion = Actual to date + To complete. These three fields are linked and by entering either At completion or Cost to complete the other two fields will be calculated.

- Scheduled Budget, Earned Value, Cost Variance, Scheduled Variance and Completion Variance are used when the schedule is statused.

 Remove the quantities (using the Resource form) after adding lump sum items to avoid them being included in histograms and tables based on quantities.

15.4 Assign Resources Against Multiple Activities

You are able to assign a resource to more than one activity by:

- selecting more than one activity,

- selecting **Insert**, **Resource Assignment** and

- then assigning the Resource by nominating the **Quantity** or the **Units per day**.

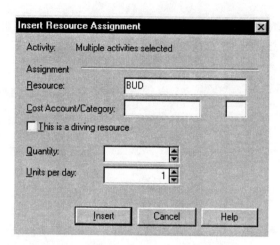

- You may assign the **Cost Account/Category** at the same time.

WORKSHOP 20

Assigning Resources to Activities

Preamble

The resources must now be assigned to the specific tasks they will work on.

Assignment

1. Use the resource detail form to assign the resources to the following activities (Lump Sum resources must be added using the Cost Detail form):

Activity ID	Resource	Units per Day	Cost To Complete
1010	TM	8.00	Calculated
	SALESENG	8.00	Calculated
1020	SYSENG	16.00	Calculated
1030	SCHED	8.00	Calculated
1040	SALESENG	8.00	Calculated
1050	SCHED	8.00	Calculated
1060	CS	16.00	Calculated
	LUMPSUM	0	150.00
1070	SALESENG	8.00	Calculated
1120	LUMPSUM	0	250.00

2. Format your columns to reflect above.
3. Group the data by Resource.
4. Check your data entry.
5. Copy this Project to a file WLB1, a new Target Schedule with resources.
6. Set this new Target Schedule as Target 1.

15.5 Earned Value Calculation

When comparing Actual Costs and Actual Quantities against Budget you have the option of choosing the Budget in the current schedule or the Target 1 Schedule.

The option is set in the **Earned Value** form by selecting **Tools**, **Options**, **Earned Value**.

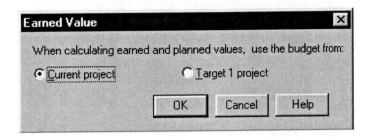

15.6 Summary Percent Calculation

The summary percent complete may be based on one of the following:

- Durations of activities

- Resource Units (for example hours or days)

- Costs

The option is set in the **Summarization** form by selecting **Tools**, **Options**, **Summarization**.

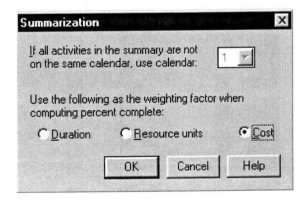

15.7 Editing Resources Calendars

Base Calendars may be applied to activities but they may not accommodate specific resource requirements. (For example when a person goes on holidays or is occupied on another project).

A Resource Calendar should be used when a resource has a unique availability.

When a resource is created a unique resource calendar is created using the base calendar entered in the Resource Dictionary. This resource calendar can then be modified to reflect that resource's availability.

Editing a Resource Calendar

The resource calendar may be edited either by:

- selecting Data, Calendars, Resource tab or

- selecting Data, Resources, Calendars.

All edits to the calendars are performed in the same manner as for the Base Calendars.

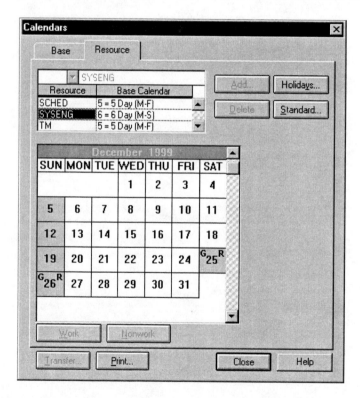

The **Resource Calendar** is a copy of a **Base Calendar**. You will need to select a Base Calendar for your resource and then edit the Resource calendar

You may then edit **Holidays** and **Standard** to create a calendar that represents the availability of your resource.

15.8 Using a Resource Calendar to Calculate Durations

A resource calendar will only be used for calculating activity durations when the **Activity Type** is assigned as **Independent** or **Meeting**. When the activity is assigned with an Activity Type of **Task** then the duration is calculated based on the task Base calendar.

Activity Types are covered in detail in the **USING ACTIVITY TYPES AND DRIVING RESOURCES** chapter.

16 USING ACTIVITY TYPES AND DRIVING RESOURCES

There are nine **Activity Types** in P3. Activity Types exist to enable the scheduler to simulate real life situations more closely. Activity Types have their own rules for calculation and should be completely understood by the user before they are used.

Some Activity Types have restrictions on the constraints that may be applied to them. For example, a Finish Milestone may not have a Start Date constraint.

The Activity Types are titled as follows:

- Task
- Independent
- Meeting
- Start Milestone
- Finish Milestone
- Start Flag
- Finish Flag
- Hammock
- WBS

This chapter covers the creation and use of all these activity types.

SureTrak supports **Topic** Activity Types. These may not be created in P3 but when you open a SureTrak project or import a MPX format project, the Topic activities are visible in P3. These activities may be deleted but not promoted or demoted or have their Task type changed in P3.

16.1 Assigning an Activity Type to an Activity

Activity Types may assigned by:

- Selecting from the **Act. Type** drop down box in the **Activity Form** or typing in the first letter in the box.
- Displaying a column with Activity Type and updating the column.

16.2 Task

Use this for scheduling normal activities. This Activity Type always utilizes the calendar assigned in the Activity Form for calculation of dates and durations.

When an activity is nominated as a Task, the Resource ignores its Resource Calendar; irrespective of whether the Resource is Non Driving or Driving.

 It is recommended that the Activity Type of **Task** be used for all work except when specific scheduling requirements dictate the need for another Activity Type.

16.3 Independent

An Activity should be made Independent when a resource is to be scheduled using the resource calendar to determine the activity duration.

The Resource should be set to **Driving** when assigned to an Independent activity.

- When a Resource is set to **Non Driving**, then it may be scheduled outside the activity duration and therefore provide a result which is not logical.

- When an activity is changed from **Task** to **Independent** then a Non Driving Resource **should** be changed to Driving. Unlike SureTrak, P3 does not change the resource from Non Driving to Driving when the task type is changed from Task to Independent.

- The Activity utilizes the resource calendar for calculating Finish dates. The Activity Start dates will be the earliest of the Driving Resources and End dates the latest of the Driving Resources.

- The resource **Lag** is the delay from the start of an activity to when a resource starts working. Therefore, when one resource is assigned to an activity with a lag then the **Lag** plus the **Duration** determines the length of the activity.

- The Resource may work independently, therefore, it may work on an activity when other resources assigned to the Activity are not available due to their own calendars.

16.4 Meeting

These are similar to Independent Activities but all resources must be available for work according to their own Resource Calendars for the Activity to have the work scheduled.

- All the resources must be Driving for Meeting Activities to calculate correctly.

- When changing an Activity from Task to meeting to Independent then Non-driving Activities **should** be changed to Driving. Unlike SureTrak, P3 does not change the resource from Non-driving to Driving when the task type is changed from Task to Independent.

The following diagram shows how P3 schedules Task, Independent and Meeting Activities.

2 Day Activity	Day 1	Day 2	Day 3	Day 4	Day 5	Day 6	Day 7
Calendar for Resource 1			▓	▓			
Calendar for Resource 2	▓						
Calendar for Resource 3	▓	▓			▓		
Activity 1 – Task	█	█					
Activity 2 – Independent	█	█	█	█			
Activity 3 – Meeting						█	█

16.5 Start Milestone

A Start Milestone has no duration and is often used to indicate the start of a major event:

- A Start Milestone only has a Start Date.

- A Start Milestone has to be statused or it will remain in front of the data date.

- Constraints which are not allowed are grayed out in the constraints box.

16.6 Finish Milestone

A Finish Milestone has no duration and is often used to indicate the end of a major event:

- A Finish Milestone only has a Finish Date.

- A Finish Milestone has to be statused or it will remain in front of the data date.

- Constraints which are not allowed are grayed out in the constraints box.

16.7 Start Flag

A Start Flag is used to calculate the Earliest Start Date of a group of one or more activities.

- A Start Flag should have a predecessor relationship with one or more activity. When the schedule is calculated it will have a Start Date at the latest of the Early Start Dates or Actual Start Dates of its predecessors.

- A Start Flag is not statused and, therefore, when all its predecessors have Actual Start dates and are in the past it will be calculated in the past.

16.8 Finish Flag

A Finish Flag is used to calculate the Earliest Finish Date of a group of one or more activities.

- A Finish Flag requires a predecessor relationship with one or more activity. When the schedule is calculated a Finish Flag will have a Finish Date on the latest of the Early Finish Dates or Actual Finish Dates of its predecessors.

- A Finish Flag is not statused and, therefore, when all its predecessors have Actual Finish dates and are in the past it will be calculated in the past.

16.9 Hammock

A Hammock is used to summaries the duration of a group of activities. It does not summaries costs or resources and is independent of the activity coding of activities it is summarizing.

To create a Hammock

- From the Activity Detail Form select Activity Type **Hammock**.

- Create a Start to Start Predecessor relationship to one or more activities that dictate the start of the Hammock.

- Create a Finish to Finish Successor relationship to one or more activities that dictate the finish of the Hammock.

Resources and costs may be assigned to Hammocks.

 Be careful with setting the Autocost Rules. When the resource is assigned as Non-driving, and units per hour frozen, the Quantity to complete will increase when the Hammock duration is increased. When a resource is made Driving it ignores the duration of the Hammock for scheduling the work.

16.10 Topic

Topic Activities are created when Outlining in SureTrak is used or when you import a project in MPX Format.

MPX is a Microsoft Project text format of project data that is commonly used to transfer data from one software package to another. Due to the differences in the software a schedule imported from MPX will not always give the same answer when calculated in P3.

Resources may be assigned to Topic Activities:

- The resource adopts the duration of the activity when assigned as **Non Driving**

- When the **Resource Unit Per Hour** is frozen an increase in duration will increase the quantity and cost.

- If the Resource is **Driving** then the resource is effectively scheduled separately to the Task.

 It is suggested that you do not attempt to use Topic Activities in P3 and they should be deleted.

WORKSHOP 21

Assigning Resources to Activities

Preamble

It is intended to demonstrate the difference between Task, Independent and Meeting Activities. We will model the table in P3.

2 Day Activity	Day 1	Day 2	Day 3	Day 4	Day 5	Day 6	Day 7
Calendar for Resource 1			▩	▩			
Calendar for Resource 2	▩						
Calendar for Resource 3	▩	▩			▩		
Activity 1 – Task	██	██					
Activity 2 – Independent	██	██	██	██			
Activity 3 – Meeting						██	██

Assignment

1. Create a new Project name **TYPE**, with a daily calendar, Start date 1 Jan 2000 and a 7-day work week.
2. Create three Resources, Resource 1, Resource 2 and Resource 3.
3. Edit the Resource calendars to reflect the availability above.
4. Create three activities all two days in length:
   - Activity 1 – Task
   - Activity 2 – Independent
   - Activity 3 – Meeting
5. Assign all the resources to each activity and schedule.

17 STATUSING PROJECTS WITH RESOURCES

This chapter covers the following subjects:

- Understanding Target Schedule and Budgets
- Understanding the Data Date
- Information Required to Update a Resourced Schedule
- Updating Dates and Percentage Complete
- Recording Progress on the Bar Chart
- Using Expected Finish Constraint
- Progress Spotlight and Progress Update
- Updating Resources
- Storing Period Actual Costs and Quantities and
- Resource Histograms and S-Curves.

17.1 Understanding Target Schedule and Budgets

Budgets

The Budget hours or quantities and costs of resources are automatically recorded in the Budget field of each resource as the resource is assigned to an activity.

Targets

A Target Schedule is a complete schedule against which your progress and performance is measured. Setting the Target schedule is covered in the **TRACKING PROGRESS** chapter.

Target dates may be viewed by the following methods:

- Display the Target start and finish date columns
- Display the **Target Bar** in the bars chart area or
- Display the **Dates** form from **View, Activity Detail, Dates**.

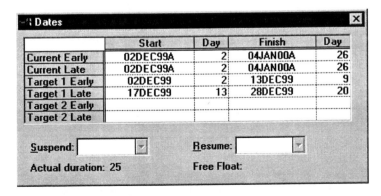

	Start	Day	Finish	Day
Current Early	02DEC99A	2	04JAN00A	26
Current Late	02DEC99A	2	04JAN00A	26
Target 1 Early	02DEC99	2	13DEC99	9
Target 1 Late	17DEC99	13	28DEC99	20
Target 2 Early				
Target 2 Late				

Suspend: Resume:

Actual duration: 25   Free Float:

There are two distinct processes when statusing a schedule:

- Statusing the dates then

- Statusing the resources, costs and quantities.

There are relationships between resources and the percent complete that may be created or broken and are governed by **Autocost Rules**. These rules must be understood to successfully status a resourced schedule. They are not easy to comprehend but these rules are a feature that makes P3 a good scheduling tool.

17.2 Understanding the Data Date

The **Data Date** is also known as **Review Date**, **Status Date**, **As Of Date** and **Update Date**.

- The **Data Date** is the date that divides past and future in the schedule.

- **Actual Costs** and **Quantities/Hours** should have occurred before the data date.

- **Costs** and **Quantities/Hours To Complete** occur after the data date.

- **Remaining durations** are calculated from the Data Date.

- The **Data Date** is not normally in the future, but often in the recent past, due to the time it may take to collect the information to status the schedule.

To modify the Data Date color select **Format**, **Sight Lines** to open the **Sight Lines** form and select the **Data Date** tab.

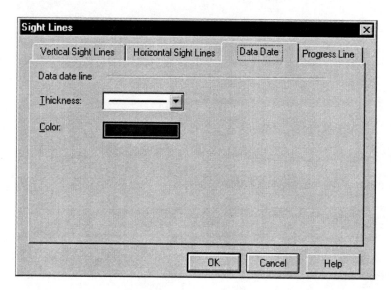

17.3 Information Required to Update a Resourced Schedule

A project schedule is usually updated at the end of a period, such as each day, week or month. One of the purposes of updating a schedule is to establish differences between the Baseline/Original Plan and the Current schedule.

The following information is required to status a schedule :

Activities commenced in the update period require:

- Actual start date of the activity.

- Remaining Duration from the status date or Expected finish date.

- Costs and Hours or Quantities to date and/or Costs and Hours or Quantities this period or Total to date.

- Costs and Hours or Quantities to complete.

Activities completed or started and completed, in the update period require:

- Actual Start date of the activity.

- Actual Finish date of the activity.

- Costs, Hours and/or Quantities to date.

Activities not commenced require:

- Changes in logic or date constraints.

- Changes in Costs or Hours or Quantities.

- Changes in duration.

Once this information is collected the schedule may be updated.

17.4 Updating Dates and Percentage Complete

Activity dates, remaining duration and percentage complete may be statused using one of three principal methods:

- Using the Activity Form, (as outlined in the **TRACKING PROGRESS** chapter)
- Using Columns
- Recording Progress on the bar chart
- Using Progress Spotlight & Update Progress.

17.4.1 Recording Progress Using Activity Form

The Activity Form may be used for statusing activities in conjunction with the **Dates** form for Suspending and Resuming activities.

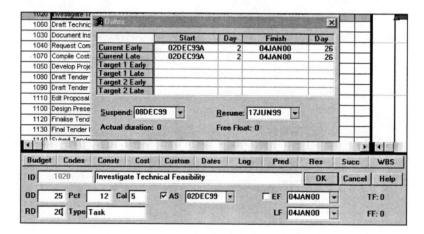

17.4.2 Recording Progress Using Activity Columns

A layout may be created with the columns required to status a project. You should display all the columns you wish to status.

Actual Start and **Actual Finish** columns are available in P3, see below.

Activity ID	Activity Description	Orig Dur	Rem Dur	%	Early Start	Actual Start	Early Finish	Actual Finish
1000	Tender Request Requested	0	0	100	01DEC99A	01DEC99		
1010	Tender Stratergy Meeting	1	0	100	01DEC99A	01DEC99	01DEC99A	01DEC99
1020	Investigate Technical Feasibility	8	6	25	02DEC99A	02DEC99	15DEC99	
1060	Draft Technical Details	9	9	0	16DEC99		28DEC99	
1030	Document Installation	4	4	0	16DEC99		21DEC99	
1050	Develop Project Schedule	4	4	0	22DEC99		27DEC99	
1040	Request Component Tenders	3	3	0	03JAN00*		05JAN00	
1070	Compile Costs From Tenders	2	2	0	06JAN00		07JAN00	
1080	Draft Tender Documents	3	3	0	08JAN00		10JAN00	
1090	Draft Tender Meeting	1	1	0	11JAN00		11JAN00	
1110	Edit Proposal Draft	2	2	0	12JAN00		13JAN00	
1100	Design Presentation	1	1	0	12JAN00		12JAN00	
1120	Finalise Tender Package	6	6	0	14JAN00		19JAN00	
1130	Final Tender Meeting	1	1	0	20JAN00		20JAN00	

17.5 Recording Progress on the Bar Chart

To record progress on the bar chart:

- Set the **Actual Start** by moving the mouse pointer to the start of the activity and a double-headed arrow will be displayed, press the **Shift** key to display the icon shown below.

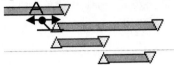

- Click with the left mouse button and drag the bar to the required Actual Start Date. You will be presented with this form:

- Click on **Yes** and you will be presented with the **Progress** form:

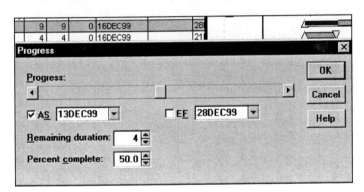

- You may mark up the **Percent Complete** using the slide or typing in the **Percent Complete** and update the **Remaining Duration**. As the percentage is increased the bar will be highlighted, see above.

Follow the same procedure to record the **Actual Finish**.

17.5.1 Using Expected Finish Constraint

You may set the **Finish Date** with an **Expected Finish Date Constraint**, and then P3 will calculate the Remaining Duration for you. Therefore, you will not have to status the activity.

The Remaining Duration will have an asterisk by it indicating that P3 has calculated the duration and, therefore, there is a **Expected Finish** date constraint.

Activity Description	Orig Dur	Rem Dur	%	Early Start	Early Finish
Activity with Expected Finish Constraint	6*	6*	0	08FEB00	15FEB00

When an **Expected Finish** constraint moves into the past and is not marked as complete with an actual finish, then this error will be noted as in the scheduling report below:

```
Constraint listing -- Scheduling Report Page: 2
Activity Date    Constraint
----------  -------  ---------------------------
2 15FEB00 Expected Finish Constraint

Bad expected finish on activity 2, this constraint will be ignored.
```

When an expected finish moves into the past the **Remaining Duration** is set to zero and **Quantities to Complete** are also set to zero. ie It deletes your ETC.

17.6 Progress Spotlight and Progress Update

These functions are used together for statusing a schedule.

- **Progress Spotlight** enables you to drag the **Data Date** with the mouse to the next period and

- **Progress Update** updates the **Percentage Complete**, **Remaining Duration**, **Resource Quantity** and **Resource Cost** to reflect what would have happened if the project had proceeded according to schedule.

You have the option of statusing all the activities or some of them. If you wish to status just some activities then select these activities before opening the **Update Progress** form.

There are two methods of setting the new data date:

- Use **Progress Spotlight** to drag the **Data Date** line with the mouse to the next end of period or

- Set the new **Data Date** in the **Progress Update** form.

17.6.1 Progress Spotlight

To use **Progress Spotlight** by dragging the Data Date:

- Set the Timescale to be compatible with your Update Periods.

- Place the mouse arrow over the **Data Date** line and it will change to the icon ⊹.

- Right click the mouse and drag the date to the end of your next period.

- The screen will look like the picture below. (Note the activities to be updated are highlighted).

Activity ID	Activity Description	Orig Dur	Rem Dur	%	Early Start	Early Finish	1999 NOV DEC JAN
Administration							
Melinda Young - Clerical Support							
1110	Edit Proposal Draft	1	1	0	14JAN00	14JAN00	
1120	Finalise Tender package	5	5	0	17JAN00	21JAN00	
Information Technology							
Scott Morrison - Systems Analyst							
1020	Investigate Technical Feasibility	8	6	25	02DEC99A	15DEC99	
1060	Draft Technical Details	9	9	0	16DEC99	29DEC99	
1030	Document Installation	4	4	0	16DEC99	20DEC99	
1050	Develop Project Schedule	4	4	0	21DEC99	24DEC99	
Purchasing							
Angela Lowe - Purchasing							
1040	Request Component Tenders	3	3	0	03JAN00*	05JAN00	
1070	Compile Costs from Tenders	2	2	0	06JAN00	07JAN00	
David Williams - Accounts Manager							
1010	Tender Stratergy Meeting	1	0	100	01DEC99A	01DEC99A	
1080	Draft Tender Documents	3	3	0	10JAN00	12JAN00	
1100	Design Presentation	1	1	0	14JAN00	14JAN00	
1130	Final Tender Meeting	1	1	0	24JAN00	24JAN00	
Sales							
Carol Pererson - Tender Manager							
1000	Tender Request requested	0	0	100	01DEC99A		
1090	Draft tender Meeting	1	1	0	13JAN00	13JAN00	
1140	Submit Tender	0	0	0		24JAN00	

To use **Progress Spotlight** by selecting **View, Progress Spotlight**:

- Set the Timescale to be the same as your Update Periods. If you are statusing weekly then set the time period to weeks in the **Timescale** form.

- Select **View, Progress, Spotlight** or click on the 🖼 icon and the next period of time (one week if your scale is set to one week) will be highlighted.

You are now ready to update progress.

17.6.2 Update Progress

Select **Tools**, **Update Progress** to open the **Update Progress** form.

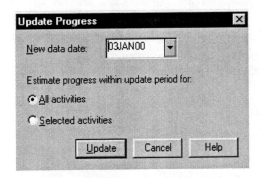

- If you have not changed the **Data Date** with the **Spotlight** function then it may be set in this form.

- Select **All activities** to update all activities or **Selected Activities** when you have made a selection prior to opening the **Update Progress** form.

- Click on **Update** to update the schedule.

- **Early start** and **Early finish** are set to **Actual start** dates and **Actual finish** dates where appropriate.

- **Percentage Complete** and **Remaining Duration** are linked during Update Progress even if you have unlinked them in the **Autocost Rules**.

- **Resource Quantity** and **Resource Cost** are updated by the new calculated **Percent Complete**. This calculates costs and quantities to date and to complete based on the **Autocost Rule "Use the update percent complete against budget to estimate"**. Though this may not necessarily be what you wanted to happen.

- Updating a Spotlighted activity before running **Update Progress** will prevent unwanted changes to activities and manually statused activity will not be changed by **Update Progress**.

- It is suggested that you may wish to create a **Custom Data Item** and copy in the last period Percentage Complete into this custom data item so you have a record of last period's percent complete to compare with the one calculated by P3.

- It is recommended that you back up your schedule before Updating Progress.

P3 **Progress Spotlight** is similar to the SureTrak **Update Progress** facility for updating a project, but there are differences:

- P3 will not reverse progress in the same way as the SureTrak **Update Progress**,

- P3 does not give you the option of not updating the resources and

- P3 will not move the Progress Spotlight more than one time period.

17.7 Updating Resources

P3 has **Autocost Rules** that allow the scheduler to decide how costs and quantities are calculated. These should be reviewed before statusing the schedule for the first time as their values often need to be different from those used when creating the initial schedule.

It is important that these options are understood. They are well defined in P3 Help and the descriptions are self-explanatory.

17.7.1 Tools, Options, Autocost Rules

Select **Tools, Options, Autocost Rules** to access the Autocost form.

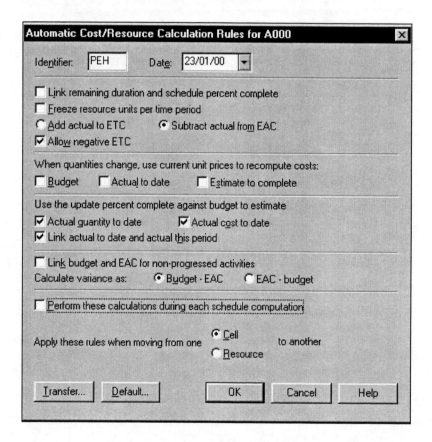

- **Identifier** and **Dates** are text boxes you may complete, but have no other purpose.

- **Transfer** allows you to transfer rules from another project.

- **Default** reassigns the default **Autocost Rules** to your project. When a project is created it adopts the default **Autocost Rules**. You may set your default Autocost rules by closing all projects and selecting **Tools, Options, Default Autocost Rules** to open the **Global Automating Cost/Resource Calculation Rules**.

17.8 Understanding Autocost Rules

Autocost rules are the single most important aspect of P3 to be understood when statusing projects with costs and resources. Individually each rule is simple, but as a group they become quite complex and it is recommended that you experiment with a small schedule to confirm that your options are giving you the result you expect before you attempt a large project.

17.8.1 Link remaining duration and schedule percent complete – Rule 1

When this box is checked the percent complete is calculated as a proportion of **Remaining Duration/Original Duration** and visa versa. When either the **Percent Complete** or **Remaining Duration** is entered, then the other is calculated.

It is recommended that this is unchecked so you are able to enter the **Percent Complete** and **Remaining Duration** separately.

It this box is checked and you set the Remaining Duration to be greater than the Original Duration the Percent Complete will be set to Zero.

17.8.2 Freeze resource units per time period – Rule 2

Checking this option results in an increase in **Quantities and Hours to complete** as the **Remaining Duration** is increased, and a decrease when the **Remaining Duration** is decreased. If this option is not checked then the **Quantity to Complete** remains constant and the **Units per hour** increase when the **Remaining Duration** decreases, and **Units per hour** decrease when the **Remaining Duration** increases.

It is recommended that this box is left unchecked so that if you increase or decrease a **Remaining Duration** the **Cost** and **Quantity to Complete** remains unchanged.

17.8.3 Add actual to ETC or Subtract actual from EAC – Rule 3

Add actual to ETC or Subtract actual from EAC

ETC is the Estimate To Complete. EAC is Estimate At Completion. This option changes the relationship between the **Actual to date** and the **To complete** resource fields.

If you do not wish the Final Forecast to increase as you enter the actual to date, then check the option **Subtract actual from EAC** and as you increase the actual to date the **To complete** will reduce to maintain a constant ETC.

It is recommended that you check the **Subtract actual from EAC**, therefore, when you enter actual costs/quantities the **Cost/quantity at Completion** will not change.

Allow negative ETC

This is useful if you wish to have a negative ETC in your project.

This may be used when you expect income or a credit to a task or when incorrect journals generate a negative expenditure which you have to reconcile against.

17.8.4 When quantities change, use current unit prices to recompute costs – Rule 4

When you assign a resource to an activity the resource cost is calculated by:

> Cost = Quantity x Resource Unit Rate.

This option allows you to unlink this relationship between Quantities and Costs.

Therefore, if you uncheck any of these boxes, you unlink the appropriate relationship in the **Budget** or **Actual to date** or **Estimate to complete** fields.

You may wish to enter the actual labor costs and hours from the payroll system; therefore you would uncheck the **Actual to date** box.

You may wish P3 to calculate the **Cost to Complete** from an estimate of hours you enter and the Resource form labor rate; in this case, you would check the **Estimate to Complete** box.

17.8.5 Use the update percent complete against budget to estimate – Rule 5

You will need to uncheck these fields when you wish to enter the Actual Quantity or Actual Cost. Otherwise P3 will calculate these fields by multiplying the % Complete by the Budget.

When an activity has Driving resources you are able to enter a Percent Complete for each resource and P3 will calculate Costs and Quantities for each resource based on the Resource Percent Complete not the Activity Percent Complete.

17.8.6 Link actual to date and actual this period – Rule 6

With this option checked, when you enter an **Actual this period**, the **Actual to date** will be calculated by increasing the original value by the value of the **Actual this period**. Or you may enter the **Actual to date** and P3 will calculate the **Actual this period**. When unchecked you may enter any figure in each field.

When the actual to date and actual this period are unlinked, the Store Period Performance feature is disabled.

 This **Link actual to date and actual this period** Autocost rule was omitted from the first release of P3 Version 3.0. It may be added to your copy P3 by loading the latest Service Pack.

17.8.7 Link budget and EAC for non-progressed activities –Rule 7

This option is usually left checked while you are creating a schedule. Any changes to the **Budget** are copied to the **At completion** fields and visa versa. Therefore, any change does not have to be made twice.

Once a project is under way this box is usually unchecked and the Budget field will not change when the EAC is altered to reflect project changes. Comparisons may then made between the EAC and Budget.

17.8.8 Calculate variance as – Rule 8

Project over runs are shown in the negative by selecting **Budget – EAC** or in the positive by selecting **EAC – Budget.**

Perform these calculations during each schedule computation.
With this box checked the Autocost rules are applied each time the project is scheduled.

When you have resources assigned to Hammock activities or activities with Finish Date constraints or Non linear resource assignment, then this option should be checked. Otherwise, the Autocost rules will not be applied to these activities when the activity durations are changed during recalculation.

17.8.9 Apply these rules when moving from one Cell/Resource to another – Rule 9

When **Cell** is selected the effect is calculated in cost and quantities immediately after you move to another cell in the resource.

When **Resource** is selected then the effect is not calculated until you click into another resource.

Beware, if at any time the Remaining Duration is set to zero the Hours/Quantity to complete is also set to zero.

17.9 Updating Resources Using Resource and Costs Forms

Select the Resources and or Costs forms to update the Resource Information.

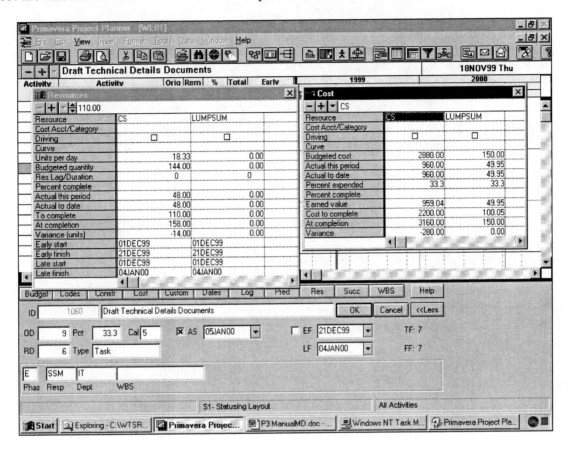

- The above example has the cost and quantities for **Actual to date** and **To complete** entered separately.

- **Percent expended** is calculated as **Actual to Date / Budget** and expressed as a percentage.

- **Earned value** is the **Budget** x **Resource Percent complete To complete**.

- **At completion** is **Actual to date + Cost to complete**.

- **Variance** is the difference between **Budget** and **At completion**.

17.10 Updating Resources Using Columns

To enter any resource data in a column you must **Group by Resource** and then costs and quantities may be updated using the columns.

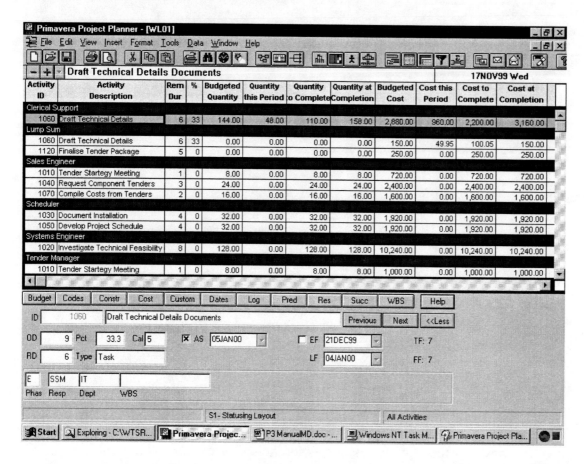

The layout must be organized by Resource to allow resource column data to be edited.

 The option to organize by Activity ID and then by Resource is available in SureTrak but not in P3. This makes finding activities difficult in large P3 schedules when organized by resource.

17.11 Storing Period Actual Costs and Quantities

This function allows you to store the actual costs and quantities for each resource and earned values in appropriate period. Therefore, actual costs and quantities which span over more than one past period will be accurately reflected in the **Resource Table** and **Resource Profile**. This facility combined with **Progress Spotlight** makes it simpler to update schedules.

The **Close Out** option in the P3 2.0 **Resource** form has been removed and is combined into the **Store Period Performance** function.

The **Store Period Performance** copies the actual quantities and costs from the **Actual this period** box in the **Costs** form and **Resources** form into the last period. The last period is defined as the period between the last two update dates and may be any period and not restricted to fixed periods.

 It is recommended that you back up the schedule before Storing Period Performance.

Select **Tools, Store Period Performance** to open the **Store Period Performance** form.

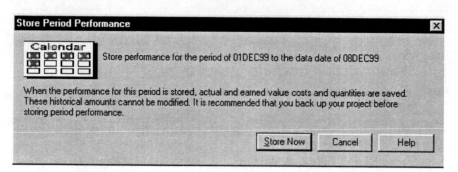

- Click on **Store Now** to store the actual and earned value costs and quantities in the last period.

- These historical values may not be directly edited.

- If you update progress incorrectly, you may correct these for the last period actual costs and quantities only by making the adjustment in the Resource Form and Cost form and then **Store Period Performance** again. This will not work for periods before the last period.

- The stored costs are spread using the calendars. Therefore, changing a calendar may alter the spread of costs and quantities on a curve.

- P3 creates a file ******HST.OUT**, with ******** being your project name which contains a history of closeout dates.

- P3 will not store data associated with an activity that has an **Actual Start** of **Actual Finish** greater than the **Data Date** and, therefore, in the future.

- If it is unable to close out any data then a text file named **CLOSEOUT.OUT** is created listing the problems. This will normally be stored in the **P3.OUT** directory.

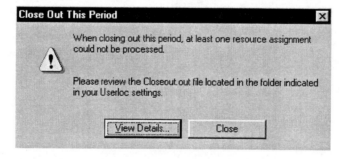

WORKSHOP 22

Updating Costs

Preamble

We need to status the activities and resources.

Assignment

1. Check the resource options and ensure that:
   - **Link remaining duration and schedule percent complete** are unlinked.
   - Both options under **Use the update percent complete against budget to estimate** are unchecked.
2. Update your project with the following data:

Activity ID	Activity Description	Actual Start	Actual Finish	Rem Dur	% Comp	Quantity to Date	Quantity to Complete	Quantity at Completion
Sales Engineer								
1010	Tender Stratergy Meeting	01DEC99	01DEC99	0	100	10.00	0.00	10.00
Systems Engineer								
1020	Investigate Technical Feasibility	03DEC99		3	40	48.00	63.00	111.00
Tender Manager								
1010	Tender Stratergy Meeting	01DEC99	01DEC99	0	100	6.00	0.00	6.00
Unassigned								
1000	Tender Request Requested	01DEC99		0	100	0.00	0.00	0.00

3. Reschedule with a **Data date** of 8 Dec 99.
4. Schedule the project and compare the current schedule to the target by producing a bar chart layout with the target bar.
5. Display the following **Additional** Columns of data:
   - Completion variance (cost).
   - Completion variance (quantity).

17.12 Resource Histograms and Tables

17.12.1 Resource Histogram

Histograms and S-Curves are not covered in detail. They may be displayed by selecting **View**, **Resource Profile** or **Ctrl F7**.

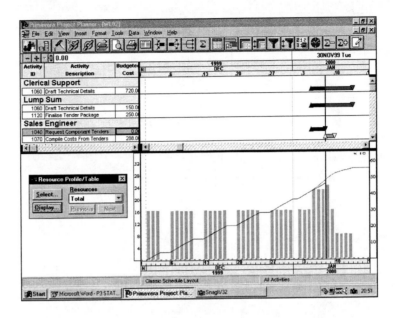

- **Select** allows you to select which resources are drawn. Resources may be grouped for analytical purposes. Use the **Ctrl** key to select more than one resource.

- Right or left click with the **mouse** over the histogram to see cumulative or period quantities or costs.

- **Display** is used to decide how the information is displayed.

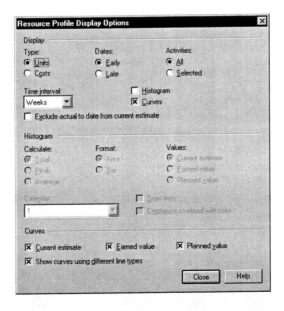

17.12.2 Resource Table

Resource Tables are not covered in detail in this book. They may be displayed by selecting **View**, **Resource Profile** or **Shift F7**.

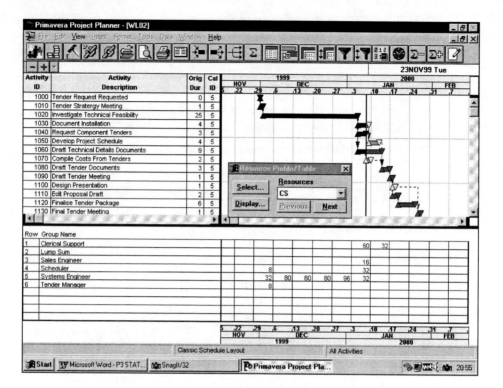

Select and **Display** are used in the same way as in the Resource Histogram.

17.12.3 Printing Histograms & Tables

Be sure you check the **Resource Cost display** in the **Page Setup** form when you wish to print a Histogram or Table.

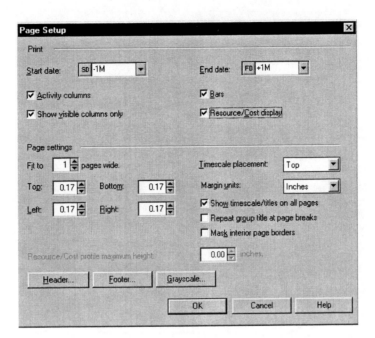

18 RESOURCE LEVELLING

Resource Leveling is a function in P3 that allows you to optimize the use of resources by delaying activities and adjusting resources to reduce the peaks in the histograms. Using this feature may extend the length of a project.

Your ability to understand how P3 operates is important if you are to utilize these options with confidence in larger schedules. You should, therefore, practice with a simple schedule to understand the complex issues of these options before leveling a complex schedule.

This chapter will outline the P3 Resource Leveling functions:

- Leveling at Project Group or Project Level
- Resource Leveling Form
- General Leveling Form Options
- Resources Leveling Form
- Prioritization Leveling Form
- Splitting Leveling Form and
- What to look for if resources are not Leveling.

18.1 Leveling at Project Group or Project Level

When the **Project Group** environment is being utilized, there is an option to prevent scheduling and leveling from the **Project Level** and only allow leveling from the **Project Group**. This option will prevent people who do not have access to the Project Group from scheduling or leveling the project.

To set the option to level at the Project Group level only or at Project Level, select **Tools**, **Schedule**, **Options**.

When the **Allow scheduling and Leveling of individual projects** option is checked, individual projects within a project group may be scheduled, without it checked scheduling and leveling may only take place at project group level.

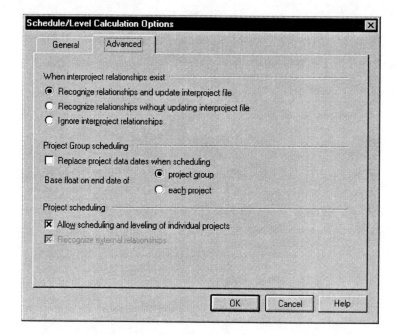

18.2 Resource Level Form

Select **Tools**, **Level** to open the Resource Leveling form.

This form is used to nominate some of the Leveling options. It is important that you review the forms **Options**, **Splitting** and **Resources** before Leveling as there are important options set in these forms.

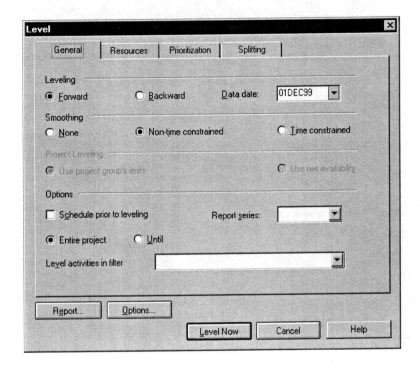

The following tabs are found in this form:

- General
- Resources
- Prioritization and
- Splitting.

Once you have set the options in all the forms, click **Level Now** to level the schedule.

18.2.1 Resource Level Form General Tab

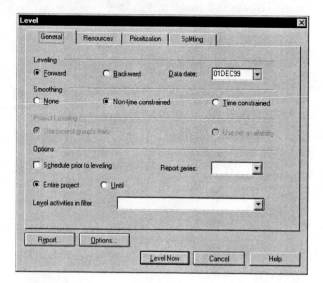

Under Leveling there are two choices, to **Forward** or to **Backward** level.

- **Forward** level commences leveling from the early dates. It selects the first activity in a network and delays the commencement of successor activities until resources are available as determined by the Resource Dictionary Limits. This produces a result that achieves the commencement of work as early as possible within the availability of resources.

- **Backward** level commences from the late start date of the last activity in a network and moves activities forward in time until resources are available. This produces a result that calculates the latest dates work may commence with the available resources.

- **Data date** allows you to reset the data date. You must check the **Reschedule prior to leveling** box prior to resetting the Data date.

   You must display the late dates to see the effect of backward leveling in the Bar Chart View.

There are three **Smoothing** options:

- **None.** consumes float and then schedules resources using the **Maximum Limits** nominated in the Resource Dictionary, and then generates **Negative Float**.

- **Non-time constrained**. This option attempts to smooth sharp increases in resource requirements that would be incurred using the **None** option.

- **Time constrained**. This option uses double the **Maximum Limit** for Leveling.

Use **Project Leveling** to control what resources limits to use:

- **Use Project Groups Limits** allows you to have full use of all of the resources within the Project Group.

- **Use net availability** allows you the use only the remaining resources after every other project has deducted its resource usage.

The simple example below shows three activities with one resource titled **RES** that has a **Limit** of "1" in the Resource Dictionary.

Before **Leveling** the Early Bar is the upper bar and the Late Bar is the lower bar.

Activity ID	Activity Description	Orig Dur	Early Start	Early Finish	Resource	Total Float	APR 17 24 1	MAY 8 15 22 29 5	JUN 12 19 26 3	JUL 10 17 24 3
100	First Activity	10	01MAY00	12MAY00	RES	55				
102	Second Activity	10	01MAY00	12MAY00	RES	55				
103	Third Activity	10	01MAY00	12MAY00	RES	55				

After **Forward Leveling**.

Activity ID	Activity Description	Orig Dur	Early Start	Early Finish	Resource	Total Float	APR 17 24 1	MAY 8 15 22 29 5	JUN 12 19 26 3	JUL 10 17 24
100	First Activity	10	01MAY00	12MAY00	RES	55				
102	Second Activity	10	15MAY00	26MAY00	RES	45				
103	Third Activity	10	29MAY00	09JUN00	RES	35				

After **Backward Leveling** (note this leveling only impacts the late bars).

Activity ID	Activity Description	Orig Dur	Early Start	Early Finish	Resource	Total Float	APR 17 24 1	MAY 8 15 22 29 5	JUN 12 19 26 3	JUL 10 17 24
100	First Activity	10	01MAY00	12MAY00	RES	35				
102	Second Activity	10	01MAY00	12MAY00	RES	45				
103	Third Activity	10	01MAY00	12MAY00	RES	55				

The other **Options** on this tab are:

- **Schedule prior to Leveling** schedules the project before leveling.

- **Report Series** enables you run a series of Tabular or Graphic Reports.

- **Entire project**. levels all activities in the project.

- **Until**. only levels activities up to the entered date.

- **Level activities in filter**, levels activities selected by a filter.

Report Form

This button opens the leveling **Report** form. You may select options for producing a leveling analysis report identifying leveling changes.

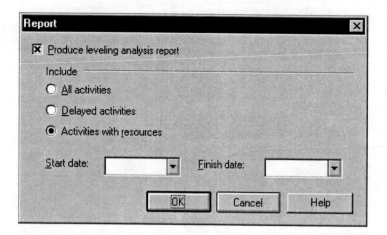

Options

This opens the Schedule/Level Calculations Options form. These options are covered in the chapter **SCHEDULING OPTIONS AND OUT OF SEQUENCE PROGRESS**.

18.2.2 Resource Level Form Resources Tab

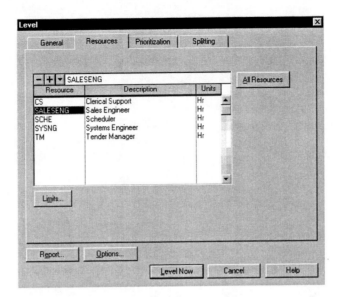

Use this form to select the resources you wish to level to the list or select click on the **All Resources** button to select all the resources to level.

18.2.3 Resource Level Form Prioritization Tab

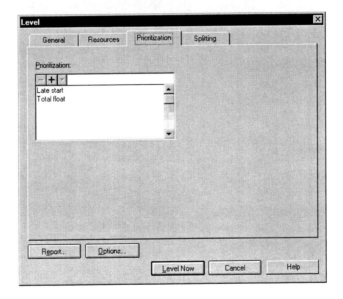

This list is used to decide which activity is delayed when two activities require the same overloaded resource at the same time. The activity with the lowest values is leveled first.

18.2.4 Resource Level Form Splitting Tab

This option allows you to select options for **Splitting**, **Stretching** and **Crunching**.

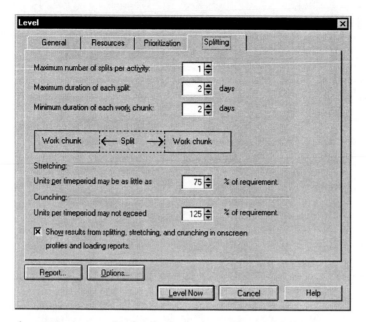

- **Splitting** enables the resource to be broken up into **Work Chunks** so that the work may be completed before and after other activities.

- **Stretching** allows the resource of an **Independent Activity** when **Forward Leveling** to have its duration increased and **Units Per Time Period** reduced.

- **Crunching** allows the resource of an **Independent Activity** when **Forward Leveling** to have its duration decreased and **Units Per Time Period** increased.

- Select the **Constraints** form to nominate the leveling method to be used for each activity.

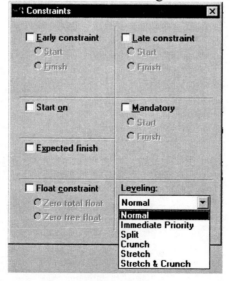

You may also create a column and use the **Fill Cell** function to assign a leveling constraint to selected activities or consider using **Global Change**.

18.3 What to Look for if Resources are not Leveling

- Have you selected resources to level in the **Resources** form?

- Have you set the **Limits** in the **Resource Dictionary**?

- Have you a **Resource Group** with the **Hierarchical Resource** and one or more resource within the group which have not be specified a limit?)which, therefore gives the group unlimited availability).

WORKSHOP 23

Resources Leveling

Preamble

This exercise is independent of the Wilson Bedding schedule. You will recreate the example in this chapter.

Assignment

1. Create a schedule titled **LEVL**.
2. Give the schedule a five-day week calendar, Start date 1 May 2000 and Finish date 31 July 2000.
3. Create three activities called First Activity, Second Activity and Third Activity.
4. Create one resource called **RES, Resource** with a normal availability of 1 and a maximum availability of 1.
5. Create the views below.

Before Leveling

Activity ID	Activity Description	Orig Dur	Early Start	Early Finish	Resource	Total Float
100	First Activity	10	01MAY00	12MAY00	RES	55
102	Second Activity	10	01MAY00	12MAY00	RES	55
103	Third Activity	10	01MAY00	12MAY00	RES	55

Forward Leveling

Activity ID	Activity Description	Orig Dur	Early Start	Early Finish	Resource	Total Float
100	First Activity	10	01MAY00	12MAY00	RES	55
102	Second Activity	10	15MAY00	26MAY00	RES	45
103	Third Activity	10	29MAY00	09JUN00	RES	35

Backward Leveling

Activity ID	Activity Description	Orig Dur	Early Start	Early Finish	Resource	Total Float
100	First Activity	10	01MAY00	12MAY00	RES	35
102	Second Activity	10	01MAY00	12MAY00	RES	45
103	Third Activity	10	01MAY00	12MAY00	RES	55

19 PROJECT GROUPS

This chapter will bring together all the aspects of Project Groups found throughout this book to provide an overview of Project Groups within one chapter.

When a new project is created in P3 it automatically becomes a **Project Group**. Sub-projects may then be created under a Project Group and these sub-projects are termed **Projects**. **Projects** share the calendars, codes, resources and other data from the **Project Group**. You may work entirely within a **Project Group** and do not have to create a **Project** under a **Project Group**.

In a corporate environment Project Groups are useful as it provides a facility to:

- Report across all projects in the Project Group.

- Analyze the total resource requirements for all projects.

- Assist in setting up new projects, as many defaults such as Calendars, Activity codes, Resources, Layouts and Reports are already defined in the Project group and available to every project in the group.

- Establish and control appropriate access to the data for each Primavera P3 and SureTrak user.

In this chapter we will cover the following topics:

- Understanding Concentric Project Management and the Role of SureTrak

- Creating a New Project

- Copying Projects

- Operating In a Multi-user Environment

- P3 Administration

- Scheduling and Leveling at Project Group or Project Level

- Autocost Rules in Project Groups and

- Project Codes.

19.1 Understanding Concentric Project Management and the Role of SureTrak

SureTrak will work with five file types:

- **SureTrak**

- is the standard format for SureTrak files and allows a maximum of 8 characters in the file name. (These files may not be read by P3).

- **Project Groups** is used when you have a number of projects sharing the same resources and must have 4 characters in the file name.

- **Concentric (P3)** is used when you wish to share the project with P3 users and must have 4 characters in the file name.

- **Finest Hour** (SureTrak Version 2.0 and earlier only) is used when you wish to share the project with Finest Hour users. Finest Hour is an MS-DOS based Primavera Program that is no longer supported by Primavera Systems Inc.

- **MPX** is a Microsoft Project text data format that many planning and scheduling software packages use to interchange data. MPP is the native Microsoft Project file format, which may not be read by SureTrak.

SureTrak may be used to open and status P3 files. They may be opened as a **Project Group** or as **Concentric (P3)** file format.

19.2 Project Group Format

Files should be created and opened as **Project Groups** in a SureTrak only environment when a Project Group and Projects environment is required.

- The Target dates are stored in columns **Target Start** and **Target Finish**.

- P3 is not able to access the SureTrak **Target Start** and **Target Finish** data.

19.3 Concentric (P3) Format

This format is designed for an environment where P3 and SureTrak are updating the project files.

- The Target dates are set in P3 when using **Concentric (P3)** format.

- The **Targets Dates** may viewed but not be saved with SureTrak.

- The Target dates viewed in SureTrak are read from the Target 1 Project set at Project level not at Project Group level date. Therefore when Project Groups are being used a Target 1 must be set in P3 for each Project.

- Users may open the file in **Project Group** format or **Concentric (P3)** format.

19.4 Differences Between P3 and SureTrak

The differences between P3 and SureTrak Version are extensive. They are documented by Primavera Systems in the help file by searching under:

- P3: exchanging data items with SureTrak,

- P3: opening and saving projects with SureTrak and

- P3: what users should know about SureTrak.

When using SureTrak and P3 in the Concentric Role you are effectively using two tools to manipulate data in a database. Each tool is able to access most of the data fields but not all of them.

The below table lists the major differences:

Function	P3	SureTrak
Layouts	Part of project file and not accessible by SureTrak	System based and path set in Tool, Options
Project Codes	Used at Project Group Level	Not accessible
Print Preview Settings	Saved with each layout	Saved as part of system, individual settings may be saved as part of reports
Autocost Rules	Total of 9 rules available	Only P3 rules 1,2,4 & 5 are recognized
Target Dates	Uses Target 1 and Target 2 files. Different Target may be set at Project Group and Project Level	SureTrak and Project Groups have columns for Target Start & Finish, Concentric (P3) draws Target from P3 Target 1 at Project Level
Topic Activities	May not be created but function in P3. They may be deleted	Created & Deleted
Outlining	Not available in Organize	Available
External Relationships	Option to Recognize	All ways recognize

Function	P3	SureTrak
Log records	99 available Not viewed in columns Viewed in reports & barcharts	First 10 only accessible May be viewed in columns
Cost Accounts Custom Data Items Resource Curves Save as Metafile Extract Activity Start date of Ordinal Dates not Project Start Date Store Period Progress Fragnets	Available	Not Available
Activity Type Flags	Available	Treated as Milestones
Resource Revenue Outlining Code Description in Columns Mixed units of Time Progress Backwards Cut & Paste from other Windows software Comment area in Project Overview	Not Available	Available

19.5 Creating a New Project

After starting P3 select **File**, **New** to create a new project. The **Add New Project** form contains important setup information for the calendars and other project defaults, such as the directory location to save the project, the project title and company name.

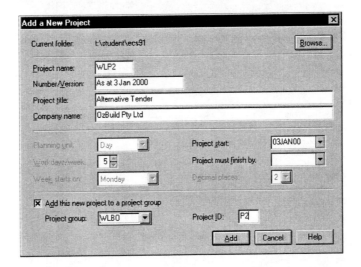

When you check the **Add this new project to a project group** box you are able to create a new sub-project or sometimes referred to as a **Member Project**. We will refer to these sub-projects as **Projects** that belong to an existing **Project Group**. You will nominate a two-character code in the **Project ID** box beginning with a letter. P3 creates a special **Activity ID Code** dictionary titled **SUBP**. This two-letter code becomes the **Code Value** in the **Activity ID.** This two-letter code identifies the project. The first two characters of each activity in one Project will commence with this **Activity ID** code.

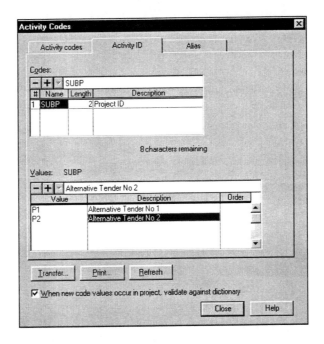

19.6 Copying Projects

Project Groups and Projects may be copied using the **Tools**, **Project Utilities**, **Copy** facility.

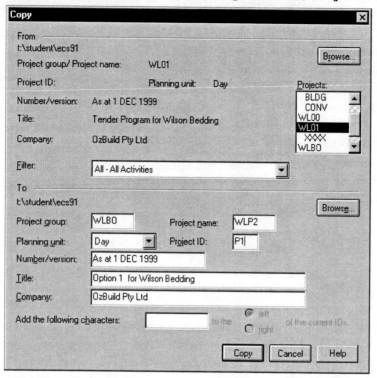

You may copy to and from Project Groups and Projects using this function.

There is an option to add characters to the left or right of the Activity ID when copying a project, (see above).

19.7 Operating in a Multi-user Environment

The book does not to cover the multi-user environment in detail. When you are working in a multi-user environment; there would normally be an administrator who would be responsible for setting up users and administering the projects. The following are important points you must understand when you are opening a project:

Select **File**, **Open** will open the **Open a Project** form.

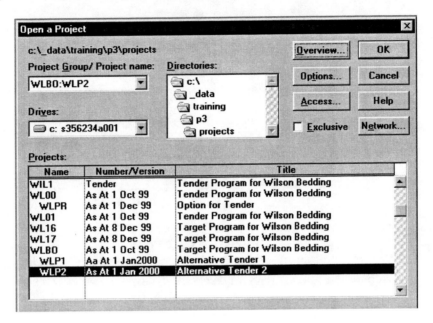

- You may select to open:
  - A **Project Group** such as WL00 or WLBO or
  - A **Project** such as WLPR, WLP1 or WLP2.

- Access nominates who is able to open the project, (this will be introduced in the next section).

- Exclusive, certain functions may only be performed when one person has Exclusive access to a project. Check this box to give you exclusive access. When more than one person is working in a Project Group you will not be able to check this box.

To see who is accessing a Project Group select **View, Current Users** or press **F5**.

 The setting of Access rights and Restrictions would vary depending on your organizations requirements. It is advised that if you have no experience in this area that you engage a competent consultant to assist you in working through these issues.

19.7.1 Access

Click on the **Access** icon to open the **Project Access** form. This is used to nominate who may open and edit the project. There are three options for each user, Read Only, Read Write and Restricted.

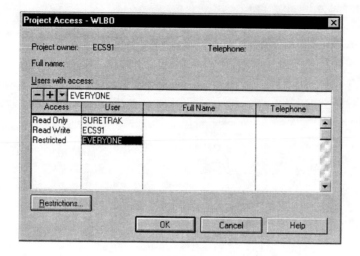

19.7.2 Restrictions

Under **Access** there is a further option **Restrictions** which is becomes available when a user is assigned Restricted Access. Click on the **Restrictions** icon to open the **Restrictions** form. This is where you define which functions the user may execute when assigned **Restricted Access** to a project.

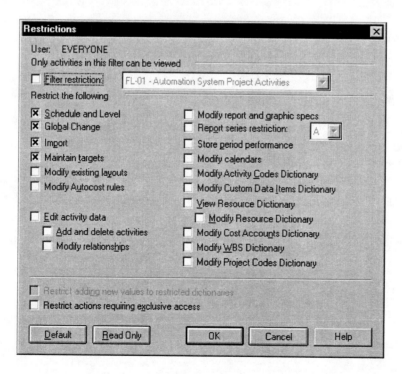

19.8 P3 Administration

In a multi-user environment there should be an administrator who maintains the system. It is important that you understand some of the basics when you are operating in this environment.

- Each user may open a maximum of four Projects from the same Project Group provided they have the necessary access rights. It is not possible to open the Project Group and one of its Projects at the same time.

- **Privileged** users automatically have access to all projects.

- The Project Owner has full rights to the project, however, a **Privileged** user may be denied access to a project by the Project Owner.

- **View**, **Current Users** lists the current users of the Project Group and their access rights.

- **File**, **Open**, **Access** is where the owner of a file specifies the access rights to a file.

- A user will require **Exclusive Rights** to a file to perform functions such as leveling and scheduling. Exclusive rights are obtained at the **File**, **Open** form.

- Users are added to a system using the **Netset** program **P3NET.EXE**. This program is the **Primavera Network Administration** program found in the **P3PROGS** sub-directory. The default password for Netset is **NETSET**.

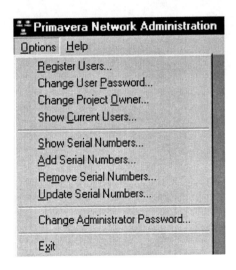

- Netset is also used to maintain the P3 serial numbers.

When in a **Concentric (P3)** environment it is recommended that the user **SureTrak** is removed from Netset thus ensuring all SureTrak users log in and are registered in Netset as users.

19.9 Project Group Autocost Rules

There may be different Autocost rules for each Member Project and the Project Group. When a project is created it adopts the **Default Autocost** rules which are defined when all projects are closed by selecting **Tools, Options, Default Auto Cost Rules**.

19.10 Scheduling and Leveling at Project Group or Project Level

Select **Tools, Schedule, Options, Advanced tab** from a Project Group and you will display the following **Schedule/Level Calculation Options** form.

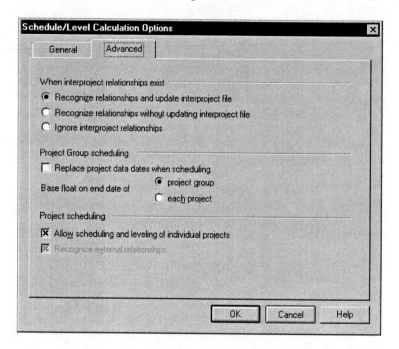

The **Advanced** tab cannot be accessed until there are Projects defined in the Project Group.

There are three sections to this form:

- Interproject relationships
- Project Group scheduling and
- Project scheduling

The last two sections give you additional flexibility for scheduling when managing a Project Group.

19.10.1Introduction to Interproject Relationships

The **Interproject Relationship Manager** enables you to create links between projects that may not be merged. This occurs when they have different **Planning Units** or have been set up differently.

This program is found in the P3PROGS with file name **INTRPROJ.EXE** and default password **INTRPROJ**.

The **Interproject Relationship Manager** looks like this:

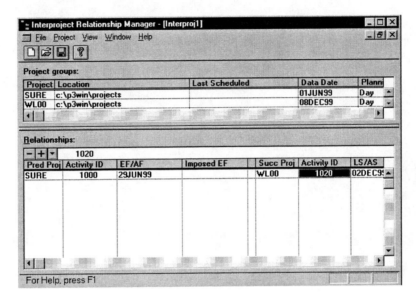

The **Interproject relationships** options in the **Schedule/Level Calculation Options** form determine how the relationships established in the **Interproject Relationship Manager** are calculated.

19.10.2 Project Group Scheduling

Projects within a Project Group may be related or they may be independent of each other. When they are related you would normally maintain one data date and schedule all sub projects together. If they are not related, then you may desire them to have different data dates and the float for each Project to be based only on that projects activities.

- **Replace project data dates when scheduling**. Check this box when the projects are related and they will be all set with the same data date. If this is unchecked then each project may have a different data date.

- **Base float on end date of**. You may show float based on the **Project Group**, which would normally be used for projects which are related, or on each **Project**, which would normally be used when the projects are unrelated.

19.10.3 Project Scheduling

When the **Project Group** environment is being utilized there is an option to prevent scheduling and leveling from the **Project Level** and only allow leveling from the **Project Group**. This option will prevent people who do not have access to the Project Group from scheduling or leveling the project.

To set the option to level at the **Project Group** level only or **Project** Level select **Tools**, **Schedule**, **Options** after opening the Project Group.

When the **Allow scheduling and leveling of individual projects** option is checked, individual projects within a Project Group may be scheduled, when it is unchecked scheduling and leveling may only take place at Project Group level.

When opening this form from a Project as opposed to opening it from a Project Group, you will be presented with different options.

Relationships between Projects are set at Project Group level. Therefore when scheduling the **Recognize external relationships** option will allow you to either:

- Schedule recognizing the relationships with between Projects of a Project Group when the box is checked or

- Ignore the relationships with other Projects when unchecked.

19.11 Project Codes

When you are operating in a Project Group environment, there are ten Project Codes that may be used for sorting, summarizing, filtering and reporting projects. Project codes are created and used in the much the same way as Activity Codes:

- Define the Project Codes dictionary, (ten per Project Group),

- Create the Project Code Values in the dictionaries and

- Assign the Project Codes to projects.

- Project Codes are used in filters organize and reports in the same way as Activity Codes.

19.11.1 Define the Project Codes Dictionary

Select **Data**, **Project Codes**, **Project Code Definition** or **File**, **Project Overview**, **Project Codes** to open the **Project Codes** form.

Select the **Project Code Definition** tab.

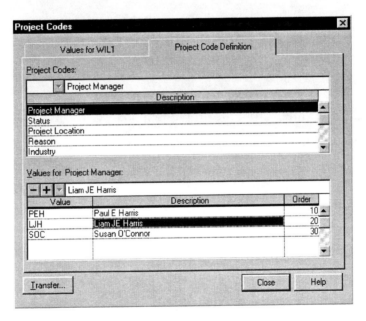

- The descriptions in the upper window may be edited to meet your organizations requirements. (The ones displayed above are the P3 default).

- Enter your **Value**, a maximum of ten characters.

- Enter the **Description**.

- Enter the **Order** if your wish to specify an order of the projects other than the default when they are displayed.

- **Transfer** will allow you to copy the codes from another project.

19.11.2Assign the Project Codes to Projects

Select **Data**, **Project Codes**, **Project Code Definition** or **File**, **Project Overview**, **Project Codes** to open the **Project Codes** form.

Select the **Values for ****** tab, ******** is your project name:

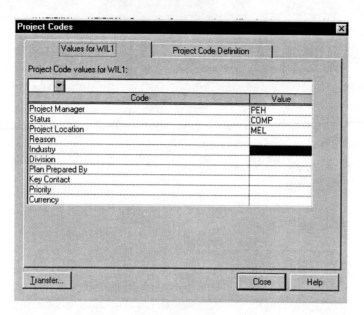

- Assign the Project Code values from the drop down box.

- **Transfer** will allow you to copy the codes from another project.

19.11.3Organizing Using Project Codes

Project Codes are used in the same way as Activity Codes and are listed at the bottom of the drop down lists.

20 TOOLS AND TECHNIQUES FOR SCHEDULING

This chapter covers some of the advanced features of P3:

Fragnets

This is a method of saving groups of activities and associated data such as Resources and Activity Codes. The activities may then be copied into any project at a later date.

Custom Data Items

You may create your own data columns and specify the data they will contain.

These are useful for holding information such as Contract Numbers, Purchase Orders, Planned Dates or additional descriptions for data.

Cost Accounts

Cost Accounts are to Resources as Activity Codes are to Activities. You may group, sort and summaries resources by Cost Accounts.

They are useful for summarizing resources under an accounting style breakdown.

Resource/Cost Distribution Curves

These allow a non-linear distribution of resources over time.

Resource Curves allow you to model the build up and tapering off resource requirements over an activity duration.

Zig Zag Progress Lines

This feature will allow you to display the progress by joining up the points with a zig zag line.

20.1 Fragnets

Fragnets are very useful when the same group of activities with their relationships, resource data and codes are required to be used multiple times in a schedule.

There are options to assign unique activity data while Fragnets are being imported into a schedule.

20.1.1 Creating a Fragnet

Fragnets are created and saved by:

- Selecting the activities to be save as a fragnet.

- Selecting **Tools**, **Fragnet**, **Store**.

- Assigning a two character ID for the Fragnet.

- Entering the Fragnet description.

- Click on **Store** and the Fragnet is saved in the P3WORK subdirectory.

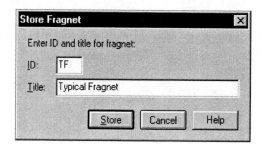

20.1.2 Deleting a Fragnet

Select **Tools**, **Fragnet**, **Delete Fragnet**:

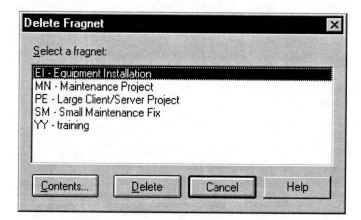

- Click on the Fragnet you wish to delete,

- Select **Contents** to see the activities contained in Fragnet.

- Click on **Delete**.

20.1.3 Retrieving Fragnets

Fragnets are retrieved (imported into the schedule) by selecting **Tools, Fragnet, Retrieve Fragnet.**

- Select the Fragnet you require from the drop down box.

- **Contents** displays a list of activities in the fragnet.

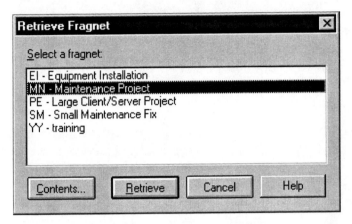

- Click on **Retrieve** to insert the Fragnet in the schedule.

- You then decide how to number the Fragnet activities with the **Paste Activities** form.

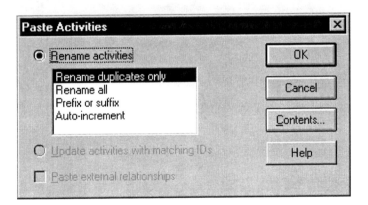

- Again **Contents** displays a list of activities in the fragnet.

- As the activities are pasted into the schedule you may be asked to confirm how Fragnet data should be treated in the current schedule. For example, should resources be added to the resource dictionary?

20.1.4 Placeholders

Some Fragnets will require additional data to be entered, such as a description, when the Fragnet is copied into a project. P3 has a facility called **Placeholders**. When you copy the Fragnet into a project you will be requested to enter the new information. Most activity data is stored in the Fragnet including Activity Codes, Resources, Constraints and Relationships.

To create a Fragnet with a Placeholder:

- Modify the activity data to include a "<" at the start of the prompt text and a ">" at the end of the prompt text and

- Then Store these activities as part of a Fragnet.

For example an activity could be stored with a description **Install <Enter Equipment Name>** and when retrieved it will prompt you to enter text to replace the Placeholder.

The **DE - Demo Fragnet** below has a place holder **<Enter Equipment Name>**.

- You will be presented with the form below to enter you your new description.

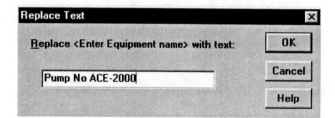

20.2 Custom Data Items

You may create up 16 Custom Data Items; 8 activity Custom Data Items and 8 Resource Custom Data Items.

Custom data items hold information in one of the following formats:

- **Character**, up to 20 characters, these may be used for descriptions.
- **Start date**, which may be displayed as a Start point of a bar.
- **Finish date**, which may be displayed as a Finish point of a bar.
- **Numeric**, from 1 to 10 digits long without decimal points
- **Precision**, from 4 to 11 digits long, which includes the decimal point and two characters after the decimal point.

The numeric and precision custom data items are summed in columns when groups are totaled in **Format organize**.

To work with Custom Data items select **Data, Custom Data Items**.

- There are a number of **Reserved Names** (listed in **Help**) that cannot be used. A warning message will appear if these are entered.
- Select the ⊞ to create and ⊟ to delete a Custom Data Item.
- Enter the **Name**, (up to 4 characters).
- Select **Type** from the drop down box.
- Enter the **Length**, (is usually the best to enter the maximum).
- Enter your Description.
- **Transfer** allows you to transfer Custom Data Items from another schedule.

20.3 Cost Accounts

Costs Accounts are codes that may be assigned to Resources and are similar to the way Activity Codes are assigned to activities.. Resources may be organized and grouped by Cost Account.

The **Cost Accounts** have two separate parts:

- **Cost Account** that may be up to 11 characters long when **Cost Categories** are used and 12 characters long when **Cost Categories** are not used. With the option of 11 or 12 characters Cost Accounts often may be matched directly with an accounting system Chart of Accounts.

- **Cost Category** that is one character long code. A maximum of 36 Cost Categories may be created. Cost Categories may often be aligned with accounting cost types.

20.3.1 Creating Cost Accounts

Select **Data, Cost Account** to open the Cost Account form:

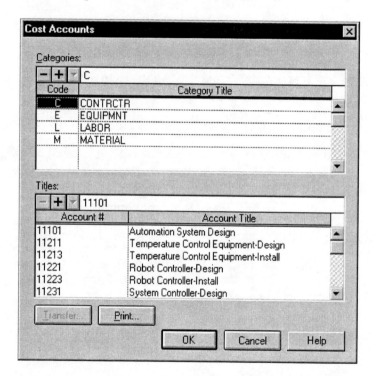

- **Cost Categories** are created in the upper window. They are assigned a Category Code and Title.

- **Cost accounts** are created in the lower window with the Account Number and Title.

- **Transfer** allows you to import accounts from another project.

20.3.2 Assigning Cost Accounts

Cost Accounts may be assigned by using:

- Columns when the activities are organized by Resource or

- The **Cost** form or

- The **Budget Summary** form.

The example below shows:

- Activities organized by **Project**, **Cost Account (11)** and **Cost Category**,

- The total cost of the project and for each **Cost Account**,

- The **Cost Account** and **Cost Category** in columns and

- The **Cost** and **Budget Summary** form.

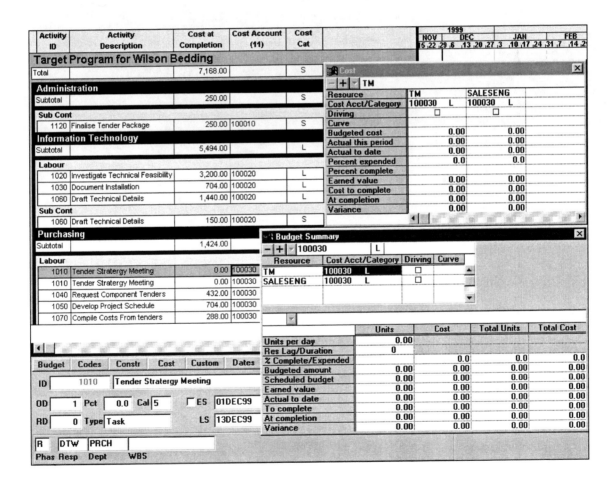

20.4 Resource Curves

Resource curves allow you to assign a non-linear distribution of your resources over time. For example, a **Bell** shape could be used to reflect a build up of resources at the start of an activity and a drop off at the end of an activity.

16 curves may be created, with a **Designator** of 0 to 9, A to F.

20.4.1 Creating a Resource Curve

Select **Data**, **Resource Curves** to open the **Resource/Cost Distribution Curves** form.

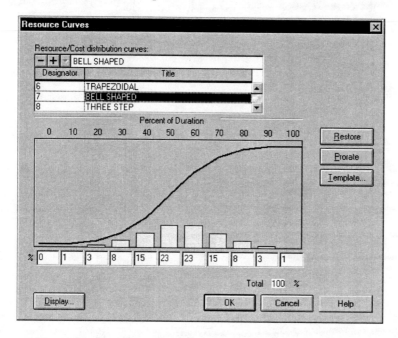

- New curves may be created by pressing the **Insert** key or clicking on the ✚ icon.

- Type in the **Title**.

- To alter the shape of the curve either type in new values in the bottom row or drag the top of the histogram with the mouse pointer.

- The **Total** will add up all the percentages. These do not initially have to add up to 100. Once you have developed the required shape you may then use the **Prorate** to adjust the percentages to total 100.

- **Restore** restores the curve to the original shape.

- **Template** allows you to create a new curve from a template. You are able to create up to 50 templates and save these in the P3.INI file.

- **Display** displays four curves at a time.

20.4.2 Assigning Resource Curves

Resource curves may be assigned using:

- **Resource** form

- **Cost** form

- **Budget Summary** form and

- **Using the Resource Curve** column.

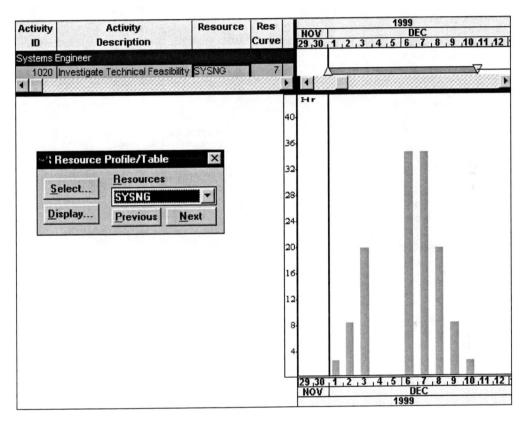

The example above shows the effect of applying a **Bell** shaped curve to the System Engineer resource on Activity 1020.

20.5 Zig Zag Progress Line

This feature will allow you to display the progress by joining up the points with a zig zag line.

Select **View**, **Progress Line** to hide or display the progress line.

Select **Format**, **Sight Lines** to display the **Site Lines** form, select the **Progress Line** tab to edit the options.

You will require a **Target** to be set before this function is available.

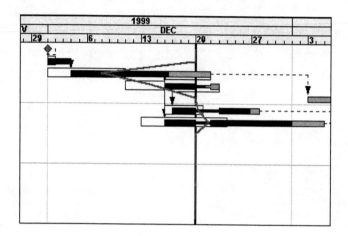

WORKSHOP 24

Reports

Preamble

You have been asked by accounts to apply some Cost Accounts to your schedule.

Assignment

1.　　Create the following Cost Accounts

Category	Category Title
L	Labor
M	Material
S	Sub Cont

Cost Account #	Account Title
100010	Administration
100020	Information Technology
100030	Purchasing
100040	Sales

2.　　Assign the Cost Accounts and create a new layout as below:

Activity ID	Activity Description	Cost at Completion	Cost Account (11)	Cost Cat
Target Program for Wilson Bedding				
Total		6,736.00		S
Administration				
Subtotal		250.00		S
Sub Cont				
1120	Finalise Tender Package	250.00	100010	S
Information Technology				
Subtotal		5,494.00		L
Labour				
1020	Investigate Technical Feasibility	3,200.00	100020	L
1030	Document Installation	704.00	100020	L
1060	Draft Technical Details	1,440.00	100020	L
Sub Cont				
1060	Draft Technical Details	150.00	100020	S
Purchasing				
Subtotal		992.00		L
Labour				
1010	Tender Stratergy Meeting	0.00	100030	L
1010	Tender Stratergy Meeting	0.00	100030	L
1050	Develop Project Schedule	704.00	100030	L
1070	Compile Costs From tenders	288.00	100030	L

21 GLOBAL CHANGE

Global Change is a facility for changing more than one data item in one step. Examples of the use of Global Change are:

- Assign resources to activities.

- Changing Activity ID's by adding, deleting or replacing characters.

- Copying data from one field to another. For example, copying the % Complete or a date into a custom data item before statusing a project. This would allow you to compare the % Complete between last period and the current period.

- Creating new activity descriptions by placing activity codes at the beginning or at the end of the original description.

- Calculate a new estimate of hours or dollars to complete, based on the current performance by using the formula:

  Estimate To Complete = Actual to Date x (100 -% Comp) / % Comp.

- Changing Calendars.

This chapter is intended as an introduction to **Global Change**. The reference manual has many examples you may review later. This chapter covers the following topics:

- The basic concepts of Global Change

- Specifying the Change Statements

- Simple Examples of Global Change

- Selecting the Activities for the Global Change

- Temporary Values and

- Advanced Examples of Global Change.

Once you understand the basics you will then develop some interesting ways of using Global change.

It is very easy to specify a Global Change that will not change data in the way you intended. You must consider your Autocost rules when using Global Change on resources, percentages complete and durations. For example, changing Original Durations will have no effect on the early Finish of activities that have commenced when Remaining Duration and Percent Complete are unlinked.

 Be careful when using Global Change, as the changes may not be undone. Consider backing up your files before making Global Changes and use the facility **Trial Run** to check your changes before making permanent changes.

21.1 The Basic Concepts of Global Change

A Global Change may be created and saved then be used at a later date.

A Global Change may not be "Undone".

Select **Tools**, **Global Change** to open the Global Change form:

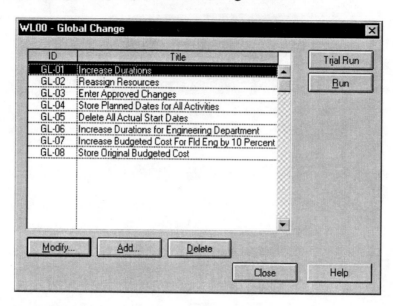

The **Global Change** form displays the list of Global Changes available in the project.

- **Trial Run** enables you to see the effects of a Global change without changing the project data.

- **Run** executes the Global Change and modifies the project database.

- **Close** closes the Global Change form.

- **Add** creates a new Global Change. When you create a new Global Change you will be required to enter a two character Alpha Numeric ID for the Global Change.

- **Modify** allows you to modify the highlighted Global Change.

- **Delete** deletes the highlighted Global Change.

 It is **STRONGLY** recommended that you always use the **Trial Run** facility to check your changes before making permanent changes by running a Global Change.

After creating Global Change using the **Add** option or selecting **Modify**, you will be presented with the second Global Change form.

This is where you select the data to be changed and where the operation to the data is specified.

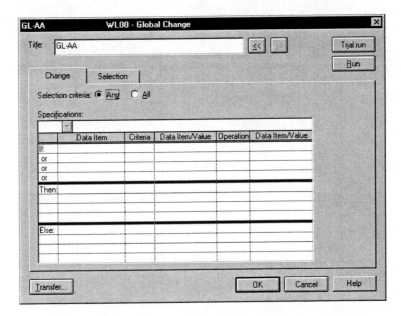

- **Trial Run** allows you to see the results of your change before changing the database.

- **Run** executes the Global Change and changes the project database.

- 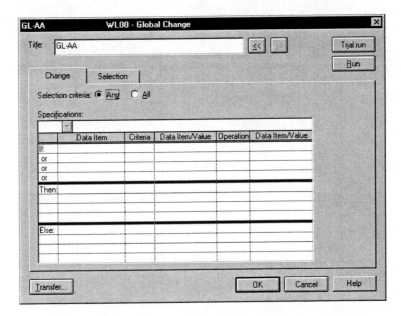 and takes you to the next or previous Global Change in the list.

- **OK** accepts your change and returns you to the first Global Change form without running the Global Change.

- **Cancel** returns you to the first Global Change form without saving changes to the Global Change.

- **Transfer** allows you to copy a Global Change from another project or the current project into the Global Change that is being edited.

There are two tabs at the top left-hand side of the form:

- **Change** displays the form where the change is specified and

- **Selection** displays a filter specification for the Global Change to allow you to nominate which activities to operate on. This option will be covered later.

The **Change** tab has three sections:

- In the four **If** lines you create a criteria for selecting the data on which to be operated.

- In the four **Then** lines you specify the operation to be applied to the selected data.

- In the four **Else** lines you have an option to specify an operation to data not selected.

21.2 Specifying the Change Statements

Then rows are used when you wish to make a Global Change to all data. There are five columns of information used to define a Global Change:

- Data Item

- Criteria

- Data Item/Value

- Operation and

- Data Item/Value - a second column with the same title.

Look at the examples on the following pages as you follow the paragraphs on this page.

Data Item

The drop down box under **Data Item** allows the selection of the data you wish to change.

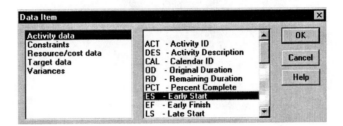

Criteria

The drop down box under **Criteria** allows the selection of the criteria you wish to use as an operand.

Data Item/Value

There are two columns with this heading.

- The left hand **Data Item/Value** column is the source data and

- The right hand side **Data Item/Value** column is target data item.

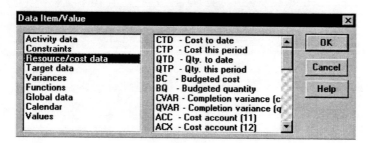

Operation

The operation defines how you want to change the **Data Item/Value**.

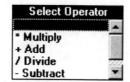

21.3 Examples of Simple Global Changes

The following examples are very simple Global Changes.

Increase Original Durations

This Global change will increase the Original Durations by 20% by multiplying the original duration by 1.2.

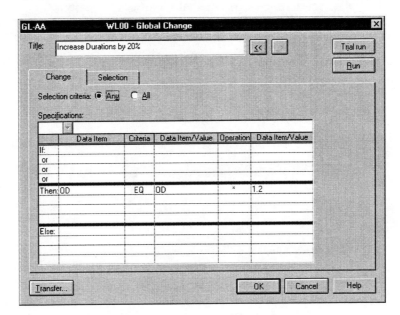

Copying Dates

This example will copy the Early Start (ES) and Early Finish (EF) into two custom data item fields Planned Start (PLST) and Planned Finish (PLFN).

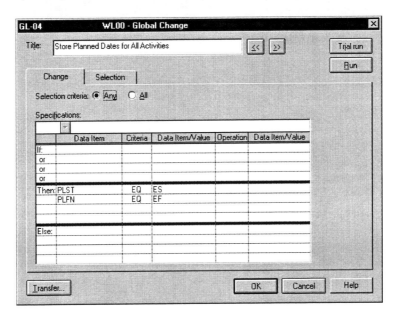

21.4 Selecting the Activities for the Global Change

Often you will want to make a Global Change to data that meets a specific criteria. The **If** statement lines are used to select the data. The operations defined in the **Then** lines will be executed. Data that does not meet the **Then** criteria may be changed with operations defined in the **Else** statement lines.

There are two facilities to select activities for Global Change Operations:

- Using the **If and Else** statement lines in combination with the **Any** and **All** radio buttons and

- Clicking on the **Selection** Tab and using the Selection feature which is identical to Filters.

If

The following example will double Remaining Durations if the percent complete is less than 50%.

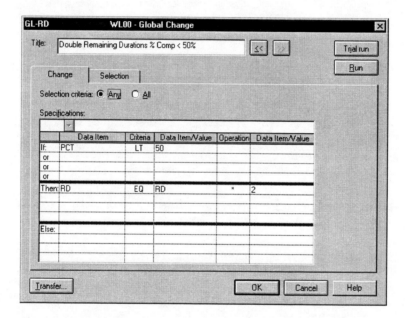

These values will only remain after schedule calculation if you unlink Percent Complete and Remaining Duration in the Autocost rules.

If and Else

The following example will add 5 days to the Original Duration of activities over 10 days long and increase those under 10 days long by 20%.

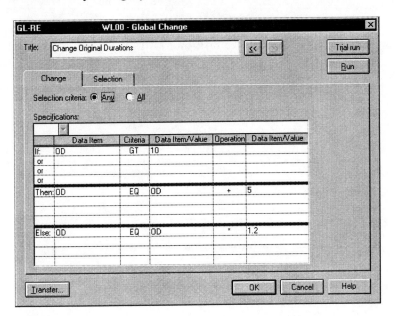

Any and All

There are two radio buttons in the center at the top of the tab, **All** and **Any**. These are used in conjunction with the four **If** statements lines.

When **Any** is selected the Global Change will operate when any of your selection criteria is met. In the example below, any activity with the Original Duration greater than 10 days or an activity that is assigned to the IT Department, IT, will be increased by 5 days.

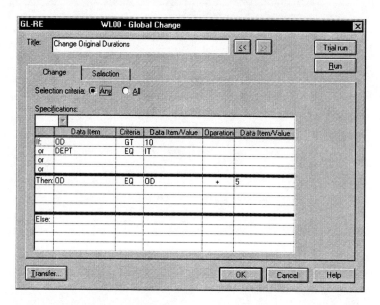

Every selection criteria has to be met when **All** is selected for the Global Change to operate on the data. In the example below only activities with the Original Duration greater than 10 days and assigned to the Purchasing Department (PRCH) will be increased by 5 days. The remainder increased by 20%.

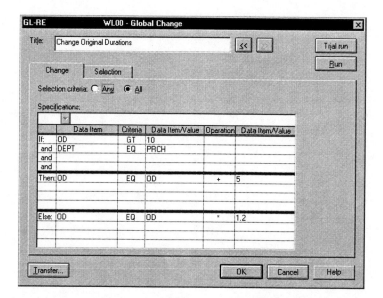

21.5 Selection

There are two Tabs at the top of the screen, **Change** and **Selection**. A screen similar to the **Filter Specification** form is displayed when the **Selection** tab is clicked. You are able to nominate which activities are selected for the Global Change. This is the same as creating a filter.

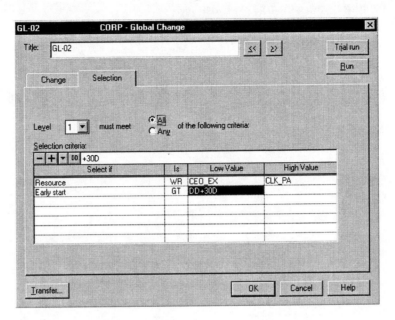

You will not need to use the **Selection** form when you are able to make your Global Change selection using the **Change** form.

The **If** and **Else** will operate on all the data that is selected in the **Selection Form**.

 When you select data by Resource or Cost Account or Cost Category using the Selection form P3 will filter on Activities that meets the criteria. A Global Change to Resources will affect all Resources for Activities filtered by the criteria in the **Selection** form. Therefore you will also need to enter an IF statement in the **Change** form to ensure only the resources you wish to be changed are changed.

21.6 Temporary Values

Some calculations require more than one operation to achieve the required change. A **Temporary Value** is created on a **Then** or **Else** line. This **Temporary Value** may then be used on a subsequent line. Any **Data Item/Value** that is commenced with an **&** sign followed by up to three characters is treated as a **Temporary Value**.

The example below is used to calculate Cost to Complete (CTC) based on a calculated unit cost calculated from the Actual Cost divided by the Actual Quantity:

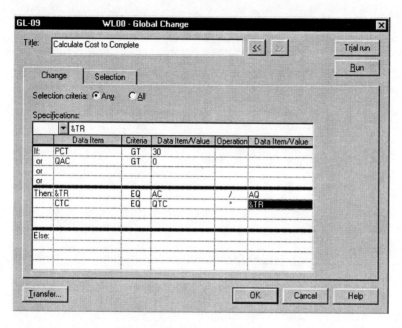

In this example AC/AQ calculates the unit rate, and the CTC is the unit rate x the QTC.

- The percent complete must be greater than 30%.

- The resource must have a quantity.

- **&TR**, a temporary value, is cost per unit calculated by dividing Actual Cost (AC) by Actual Quantity (AQ).

- Cost to Complete (CTC) is equal to Quantity to Complete (QTC) multiplied by **&TR**.

21.7 Adding and Deleting Resources

Global Change may be used to add or delete resources from activities.

Adding Resources with Global Change

The example below assigns a resource Clerical Support **CS** at 2 units per time period **UPT** to all activities in the Purchasing Department **PRCH**.

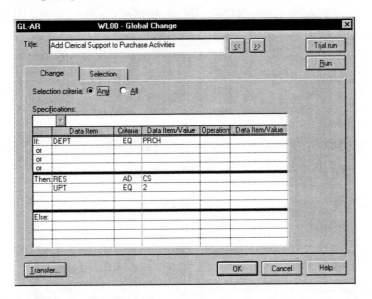

Deleting Resources with Global Change

To delete a resource select it with the **IF** statement and delete it in the **Then** statement by making the resource equal to **DELETE**.

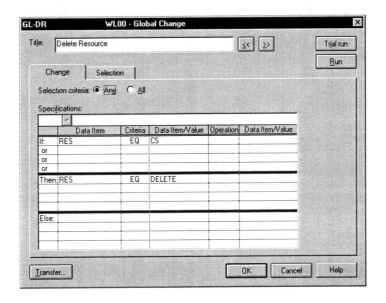

 Deleting a resource from a dictionary deletes the resource from all activities.

21.8 Global Change Functions

There are a number of functions that may be used in conjunction with Global Change. These are covered in detail in the Primavera Project Planner Reference Manual and Help. The list is intended as a guide to the functions available.

Dates

Dates are stored as numbers and displayed as dates. Therefore you are able to create new dates by adding or subtracting numbers from dates or dates from dates:

- 25MAY99 – 23MAY99 = 2

- ES + 4 = 26MAY99

- T1EF – EF = 2

String Functions

A string may be a description, an activity code or a resource name. The following functions may be used in Global Change to edit, change or select characters in a string:

RIGHT	is used to select the last few characters in a string. **RIGHT(DES,4)** selects the last four characters in the description.
LEFT	is used to select the first few characters in a string. **LEFT(ACT,2)** selects the first two characters in the Activity ID
SS	selects characters in the middle of a string. **SS(ACT,3,2)** selects two characters starting at the third character.
TTL	is used to replace data in one field with data from another field. **DES EQ TLL(RES)** replaces the activity description with resource name.
RTRIM	removes training blanks.
LTRIM	removes leading blanks from a string. (This is useful when working with a numeric Activity ID as P3 right aligns numeric activity ID's with blanks which often have to be removed before they are operated on.
STDATE	converts a date to a text string. (It may then be placed in a description).
DAY	identifies the day of a week on which a date falls on.
DATE	This is used to give the system date.

Concatenation

The ampersand character "**&**" is used to join two strings, e.g.: the following Global Change will add the Phase Name to the end of the Activity Description.

	Data Item	Criteria	Data Item/Value	Operation	Data Item/Value
If:					
or					
or					
or					
Then:	DES	EQ	DES	&	PHAS

22 OBJECT LINKING AND EMBEDDING

P3 supports OLE, Object Linking and Embedding.

You may place an object such as a table or graph from Excel, a picture or text in the Bar Chart area using the Paste function.

A **Linked** object is linked to the original file, then any changes to the original file are reflected in the Object displayed in the Bar Chart area.

An object becomes part of the P3 file when it is **Embedded** in the Bar Chart area and may only be edited by opening the P3 file and editing the Object from P3.

The commands associated with objects covered in this chapter are:

- View, Attachment Tools
- View, Objects
- Insert, Object
- Edit, Paste
- Edit, Find Objects
- Edit, Object
- Edit, Paste Link and
- Edit, Links.

22.1 View, Attachment Tools

Select **View**, **Attachment Tools** to display the tools form. This allows you to place objects on the Bar Chart shown in the example below:

- An object, the Australian Flag, is placed by clicking on the ▨ icon.

- A vertical line, running through the "a" of "an" by clicking on the ▨ icon.

- A vertical shaded area, by clicking on the ▨ icon.

- Some text, by clicking on the T icon.

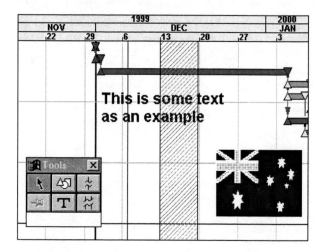

These objects may be selected by clicking on the ▨ icon and selecting the object to be edited or deleted.

Clicking on the ▨ opens the **Attachment Configuration** form. This is used to attach an object to an Activity ID or Group tiles.

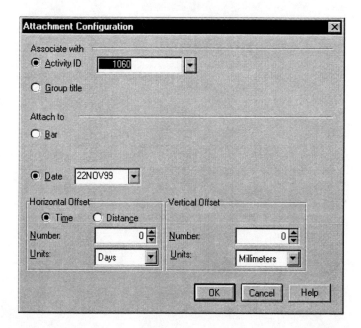

22.2 View, Objects

This option either displays or hides objects on a layout.

22.3 Insert, Object

This option is for inserting an **Embedded** object. It will open the **Insert Object** form and you may select the application you wish to use to create the object.

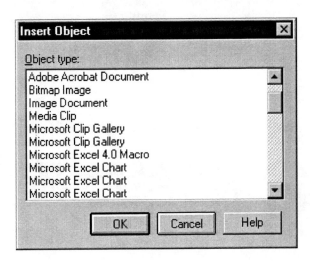

22.4 Edit, Paste

This allows you to paste an object that has been stored in the clipboard after it has been copied in another application.

22.5 Edit, Find Objects

This option opens the **Find Objects** form.

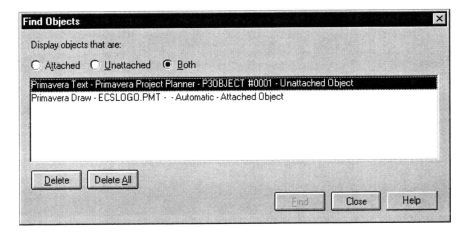

22.6 Edit, Object

You may edit objects by double clicking on them after the **Attach Tools** form has been displayed or using **Edit**, **Objects**.

22.7 Edit, Paste Link

Edit, **Paste Link** allows you to paste an object with a link to its source file. When you paste an object, the **Attachment Tools** box will be displayed. Double clicking on a linked object with the **Attachment Tools** box displayed will start the original application and allow you to edit the object.

22.8 Edit, Links

Edit, **Links** opens the **Links** form.

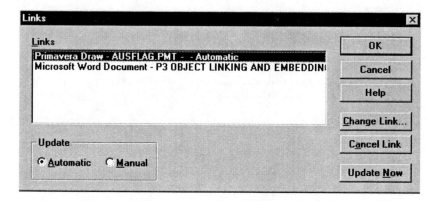

There are a number of options for updating and changing the links for objects.

23 PROJECT UTILITIES

Under **Tools**, **Project Utilities** the following options are available:

- Back Up
- Restore
- Delete and
- Check-in/Check-out.

We will also examine the following features in this chapter:

- Import and export
- Working with SureTrak version 2.0
- Batch
- PFX
- And Working with MPX files

23.1 Back-up

This allows projects to be backed up to floppy disks or to other sub-directories on the PC or Network. Projects are backed-up with your layouts.

Compress allows file compression, resulting in a single file per project with a PRX file extension.

Remove Access List, removes security restrictions on a P3 file so that it may be opened by anyone.

23.2 Restore

This restores backed-up files.

23.3 Delete

This deletes a project and ensures all files are deleted.

23.4 Check-in/Check-out

This is an option utilized with Project Groups. It is used to take a copy of a project to a remote location, make changes to the project and then return the project back to the project group at a later date. A warning message is give to any person who opens the file from the Project Group, informing them that the Project has been booked out. A record is kept of who and when files were checked out.

23.5 Import and Export

Import will import data in Lotus 123 WKS, Lotus WK1 and dBase III dbf format. **Export** allows you to export Text, Lotus 123 WKS, Lotus WK1 and dBase III dbf format. Excel will save and open files saved in all these formats.

Should you wish to import data into a P3 file it is suggested that you:

- export one or more activities in dbf format
- open the file with Excel
- add the additional data to be imported
- extend the name range "Database" to include all the data
- backup your project and
- import the data.

It is often easier to cut and paste data from spread sheets into SureTrak and then open the file with P3, but some data may not be cut and pasted in such as costs and these need to be imported.

23.6 Working with SureTrak Files

SureTrak files may be opened by P3 when they are saved from SureTrak in Concentric (P3) or Project Group format. The SureTrak Target Dates set in Project Group format will not be read by P3.

 When it is intended to open a SureTrak schedule in P3 then an 8 hours day calendar should be selected. This is because the task durations are divided by 8 when the project is opened in P3. If a project has a 10 hour day and is opened in P3 the durations will be increased by 25%.

23.7 Batch

Batch is used to import text files into P3 or to fix serious problems with a P3 file. Refer to the prmbatch.hlp file in the P3PROGS folder for details on using Batch or search on **Error** or **Batch** and scroll down to **Using batch to recover damaged files** in the P3 help files.

23.8 PFX

PFX is a Recovery Utility that may be run after system crashes to validate the integrity of the P3 files. Refer to the pfxw.hlp file in the P3PROGS folder for further details.

If your schedule gives you strange results run PFX, as this usually fixes such problems.

23.9 Working With Microsoft Project MPX Files

MPX is a Microsoft Project text format that is created by many planning and scheduling packages to exchange data. An MPX file may not be opened by P3 but may be converted to P3 format by:

- MPX Conversion Utility found under **Tools MPX Conversion Utility** or

- **Pipe**, which is an older tool used with earlier versions of P3. This has a number of options that may provide a better import because you are able to nominate specific data in the Microsoft Project Text Columns to become specific data in the P3 schedule. These facilities are not available in MPX conversion. Pipe is not part of a standard install but is available on some P3 CDs.

- Opening the file with SureTrak and saving it in P3 format.

Importing MPX files is always difficult, especially when they have been statused:

- Ensure that all Actual start dates in Microsoft Project which are before the Data Date are marked as Started. (Microsoft project allows activities in the past that have not started).

- It is recommended that you enter your P3 Activity Codes in Microsoft Project Text columns before you import the file. These are often adopted from the Outline levels.

- Never import an MPX file into a project that is part of a Project Group as it will delete all your activity codes.

- It is recommended that you remove all Topic Activities by promoting ALL activities to Outline Level 1 and deleting redundant Parent Activities. You will need to check that all logic is at the lowest Outline Level before promoting activities

- After an MPX file is imported you may wish to change the Milestones which are imported as Start Milestones to Finish Milestones, (don't forget to change predecessors from FS to FF).

- There are many other issues involved with importing a MS Project file, especially when importing resources. You may need to rename your resources in MS Project and then re-import the file to achieve your desired result. In MS Project calendars may only be placed against resources, you may wish to place calendars against activities after importing which often makes more sense.

24 WHAT'S NEW IN P3 VERSION 3.0

This chapter combines all the new features of P3 Version 3.0 in one chapter. The following is a list of the enhancements released in P3 Version 3.0:

- Assign Resources Against Multiple Activities

- Format of Individual Bars

- Automatic Scheduling and Leveling

- Enhanced Display of Activity Columns

- Timescale Pert

- Customizable Headers and Footers

- Zig Zag Progress Line

- Progress Spotlight and Progress Update

- Storing Period Actual Costs and Quantities

- Project Codes for organizing and filtering Project in Project Groups

- Primavera Post Office enhancements and

- Infomaker.

24.1 Assign Resources Against Multiple Activities

You are able to assign a resource to more than one activity by:

- Selecting more than one activity

- Selecting **Insert**, **Resource Assignment** and

- Assigning the Resource by nominating the **Quantity** or the **Units per day.**

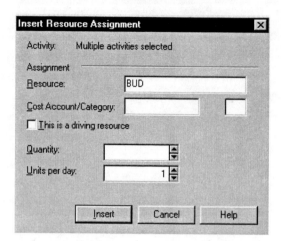

- You may assign the **Cost Account/Category** at the same time.

24.2 Format of Individual Bars

You may format individual bars by changing the color, bar type, endpoints and flag shapes. You may:

- Format one or more bars then
- Copy that format to other bars and
- Reapply the original format.

24.2.1 Format One or More Bars

To format one or more bars:

- Select the bar or bars you wish to forma and,
- Select **Format, Selected Bars, Modify Bar Format**, to open the **Format Select Bars** form:

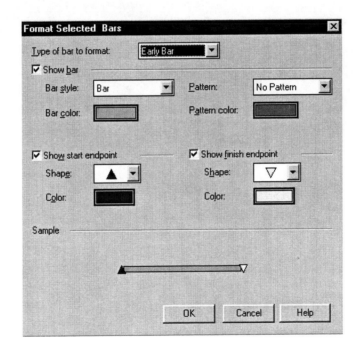

- Select the bar you wish to format from the **Type of bar to format,**(the drop down box at the top of the form).
- Uncheck the **Show Bar, Show start point** and/or **Show finish point** boxes to hide the bar, start or end points.
- Select any of the other parameters as required.
- Click **OK** to apply the formatting.
- Parameters that display **Critical** or **Progress** will overlay any individual bar formatting.

24.2.2 Copy and Paste Bar Format

Copy Bar Format and **Paste Bar Format** allows you to copy and paste a format from one bar to one or more bars.

24.2.3 Reapply the original format

Use select **Format**, **Selected Bars**, **Use Default Bars Format** to reapply the default bar format settings.

24.3 Automatic Scheduling and Leveling

P3 now has an Automatic Scheduling and Leveling Option. The project will be scheduled and/or leveled as appropriate when data is changed.

Select **Tools**, **Schedule**, **Options** icon to open the **Schedule/Level Calculations Options** form:

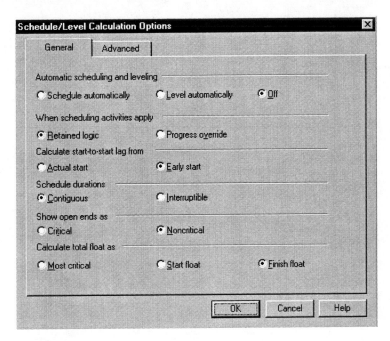

- Select **Off** and P3 will only schedule when you press **F9** or select **Tools**, **Schedule**, **Schedule Now** or click on the icon on the Tool Bar.

- Select **Schedule automatically** and P3 will schedule each time data that affects that timing (such as durations, constraints and logic) is changed.

- Select **Level automatically** and P3 will level the schedule each time you make changes to resources and recalculate the schedule.

> *i*   It is recommended that when you have a large number of activities in a schedule that you switch off Automatic Scheduling and Leveling. Otherwise you will be waiting for a period of time after each entry while the program calculates the schedule.

24.4 Enhanced Display of Activity Columns

Activity Columns now display all the resources in a column.

Predecessor and successor information may now be displayed including the driving relationships which are indicated with an *.

Activity ID	Activity Description	Resource ID	Predecessors	Successors
1000	Tender Request Requested			1010
1010	Tender Stratergy Meeting	TM, SALESENG	1000	1020*
1020	Investigate Technical Feasibility	SYSNG	1010*	1030*, 1040, 1060*
1030	Document Installation Requirements	SCHE	1020*	1050*
1040	Request Component Tenders	SALESENG	1020	1070*
1050	Develop Project Schedule	SCHE	1030*	1080
1060	Draft Technical Details Documents	CS, LUMPSUM	1020*	1080
1070	Compile Costs From tenders	SALESENG	1040*	1080*
1080	Draft Tender Documents		1050, 1060, 1070*	1090*
1090	Draft tender Meeting		1080*	1100*, 1110*
1100	Design Presentation		1090*	1120*
1110	Edit Proposal Draft		1090*	1130
1120	Finalise Tender Package	LUMPSUM	1100*	1130*
1130	Final Tender Meeting		1110, 1120*	1140*
1140	Submit Tender		1130*	

24.5 Timescale PERT

A Timescaled PERT is available which presents the activities within a timescale.

From the Pert View select **Format organize** to open the **Organize** form and select the **Arrangement** tab:

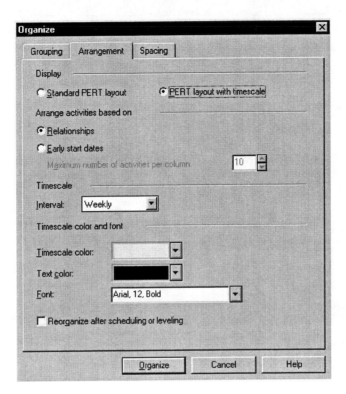

You may select the Standard PERT layout or the PERT layout with timescale.

Standard PERT layout

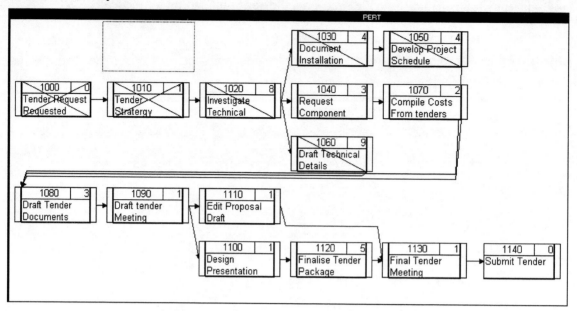

PERT layout with timescale

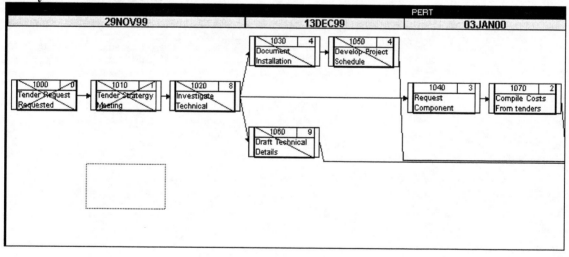

24.6 Customizable Headers and Footers

P3 now has customizable headers and footers. The formatting of the header and footer are the same.

The header and footer may be divided into 3 or 5 sections across and in each section you are able to nominate one of five types of data:

- A graphics file for displaying a picture such as your company logo,

- Titles and comments where you may select project data such as the Company Name or type in text,

- Define a Revision Box following a standard engineering format,

- Display a selection of dates including Start date, Finish date, Data date and Target dates and

- Display the bar legend.

Select **File**, **Page Setup**, **Header** or **Footer** or access **Page Setup** through print preview.

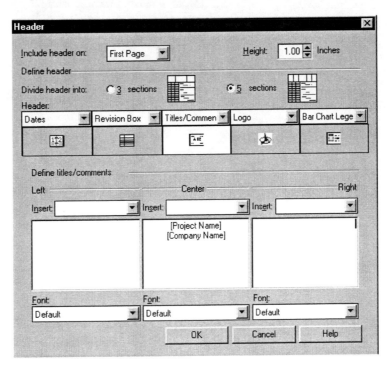

- The options are very intuitive and will not be covered in detail in this summary.

24.7 Zig Zag Progress Line

This feature will allow you to display the progress by joining up the points with a zig zag line.

Select **View**, **Progress Line** to hide or display the progress line.

Select **Format**, **Sight Lines** to display the **Site Lines** form. Select the **Progress Line** tab to edit the options.

You will require a **Target** to be set before this function is available.

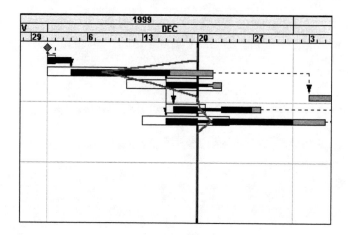

24.8 Progress Spotlight and Progress Update

These functions are used together for statusing a schedule.

- **Progress Spotlight** enables you to move the **Data Date** with the mouse to the next period highlight and the activities that should have been in progress.

- **Progress Update** updates the **Percentage Complete**, **Remaining Duration**, **Resource Quantity** and **Resource Cost** to reflect what would have happened if the project was going according to schedule.

You have the option of statusing all the activities or selecting some of them. If you wish to status just some then activities then select them before opening the **Update Progress** form.

There are two methods of setting the new data date:

- Use **Progress Spotlight** to drag the **Data Date** line with the mouse to the next end of period or

- Set the new **Data Date** in the **Progress Update** form.

24.8.1 Progress Spotlight

To use **Progress Spotlight** by dragging the Data date:

- Set the Timescale to be compatible with your Update Periods.

- Place the mouse arrow over the **Data Date** line and it will change to a ⇮.

- Right click the mouse and drag the date to the end of your next period.

- The screen will look like the picture below.

- Note that the activities to be updated are highlighted.

Activity ID	Activity Description	Orig Dur	Rem Dur	%	Early Start	Early Finish	1999
Administration							
Melinda Young - Clerical Support							
1110	Edit Proposal Draft	1	1	0	14JAN00	14JAN00	
1120	Finalise Tender package	5	5	0	17JAN00	21JAN00	
Information Technology							
Scott Morrison - Systems Analyst							
1020	Investigate Technical Feasibility	8	6	25	02DEC99A	15DEC99	
1060	Draft Technical Details	9	9	0	16DEC99	29DEC99	
1030	Document Installation	4	4	0	16DEC99	20DEC99	
1050	Develop Project Schedule	4	4	0	21DEC99	24DEC99	
Purchasing							
Angela Lowe - Purchasing							
1040	Request Component Tenders	3	3	0	03JAN00*	05JAN00	
1070	Compile Costs from Tenders	2	2	0	06JAN00	07JAN00	
David Williams - Accounts Manager							
1010	Tender Stratergy Meeting	1	0	100	01DEC99A	01DEC99A	
1080	Draft Tender Documents	3	3	0	10JAN00	12JAN00	
1100	Design Presentation	1	1	0	14JAN00	14JAN00	
1130	Final Tender Meeting	1	1	0	24JAN00	24JAN00	
Sales							
Carol Pererson - Tender Manager							
1000	Tender Request requested	0	0	100	01DEC99A		
1090	Draft tender Meeting	1	1	0	13JAN00	13JAN00	
1140	Submit Tender	0	0	0		24JAN00	

Progress Spotlight may be also used by selecting **View**, **Progress Spotlight:**

- Set the Timescale to be the same as your Update Periods, if you are statusing weekly then set the time period to weeks in the **Timescale** form.

- Select **View**, **Progress Spotlight** or click on the [icon] icon and the next period of time (one week if your scale is set to one week) will be highlighted.

You are now ready to update your progress.

24.8.2 Update Progress

Select **Tools**, **Update Progress** to open the **Update Progress** form:

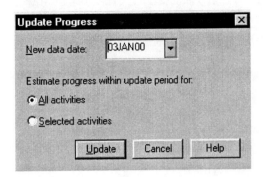

- If you have not changed the **Data Date** with the **Spotlight** function, then it may be set in this form.

- Select **All activities** to update all activities or **Selected activities** when you have made a selection prior to opening the **Update Progress** form.

- Click on **Update** to update the schedule.

- **Early start** and **Early finish dates** are set to **Actual Start** and **Actual Finish** where appropriate.

- **Percentage Complete** and **Remaining Duration** are linked during **Update Progress** even if you have unlinked them in the **Autocost Rules**.

- **Resource Quantity** and **Resource Cost** are updated by the new calculated **Percent Complete**. This calculates costs and quantities to date and to complete based on the **Autocost Rule "Use the update percent complete against budget to estimate"**. This however may not necessarily be what you wanted to happen.

- Updating a Spotlighted activity before running **Update Progress** will prevent unwanted changes to activities and a manually statused activity will not be changed by **Update Progress.**

- It is suggested that you may wish to create a **Custom Data Item** and copy the last period Percentage Complete into this custom data item so you have a record of last period's percent complete to compare with the one calculated by P3.

- It is recommended that you back up your schedule before Updating Progress.

P3 Progress Spotlight is similar to the SureTrak Update Progress facility for updating a project, but there are some differences:

- P3 will not reverse progress in the same way as the SureTrak Update Progress,

- P3 does not give you the option of not updating the resources and

- P3 will not move the Progress Spotlight more than one time period.

24.9 Storing Period Actual Costs and Quantities

This function allows you to store the actual costs and quantities for each resource and earned values in appropriate period. Therefore, actual costs and quantities which span over more than one past period will be accurately reflected in the **Resource Table** and **Resource Profile.** This facility combined with **Progress Spotlight** makes it simpler to update schedules.

The **Close Out** option in the P3 2.0 **Resource** form has been removed and is combined with the new function.

The **Store Period Performance** copies the actual quantities and costs from in the **Actual this period** box in the **Costs** form and **Resources** form into the last period. The last period is defined as the period between the last two update dates and may be any period and not restricted to fixed periods.

It is recommended that you backed-up the schedule before Storing Period Performance.

Select **Tools**, **Store Period Performance** to open the **Store Period Performance** form.

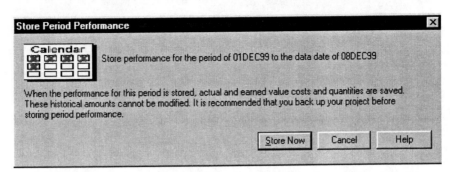

- Click on **Store Now** to store the actual and earned value costs and quantities in the last period.

- These historical values may not be directly edited.

- If you update progress incorrectly, you may correct the last period actual costs and quantities by making the adjustment in the Resource Form and Cost form and then **Store Period Performance** again. This will not work for periods before the last period.

- The stored costs are spread using the calendars. Therefore, changing a calendar may alter the spread of costs and quantities on a curve.

- P3 creates a file ******HST.OUT** containing an audit trail of Close Out Dates.   ******** is your project name. This will normally be stored in the **PROJECTS** directory, which is nominated in the P3.INI file.

- P3 will not store data associated with an activity that has an **Actual Start** of **Actual Finish** greater than the **Data Date** and, therefore, in the future.

- If P3 is unable to close out any data, then a text file named **CLOSEOUT.OUT** is created listing the problems. This file is saved in your Userloc directory, which is nominated in the P3.INI file. This is normally the **P3.OUT** directory.

-

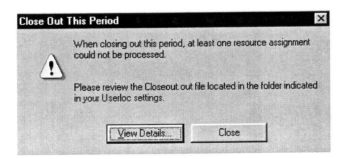

24.10 Project Codes

When you are operating in a Project Group environment there are ten Project Codes that may be used for sorting, summarizing, filtering and reporting projects. Project codes are created and used in the same way as Activity Codes:

- Define the Project Codes dictionary, a maximum of ten per Project Group,

- Create the Project Code Values in the dictionaries,

- Assign the Project Codes to projects and

- Use the codes in filters organize and reports.

24.10.1 Define the Project Codes Dictionary

Select **Data**, **Project Codes**, **Project Code Definition** or **File**, **Project Overview**, **Project Codes** to open the **Project Codes** form and select the **Project Code Definition** tab:

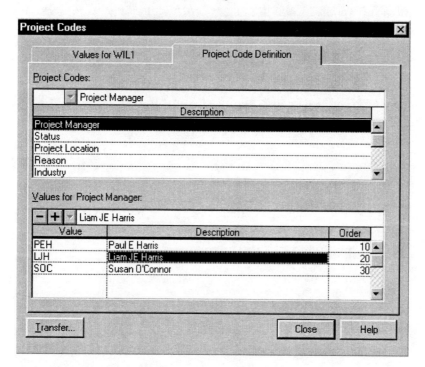

- The descriptions in the upper window may be edited to meet your organizations requirements. The ones displayed above are the P3 default.

- Enter your **Value**, a maximum of ten characters.

- Enter the **Description**.

- Enter the **Order** if your wish to specify an order of the projects other than the default when they are displayed.

- **Transfer** will allow you to copy the codes from another project.

24.10.2 Assign the Project Codes to Projects

Select **Data**, **Project Codes**, **Project Code Definition** or **File**, **Project Overview**, **Project Codes** to open the **Project Codes** form.

Select the **Values for ****** tab, ******** being your project name:

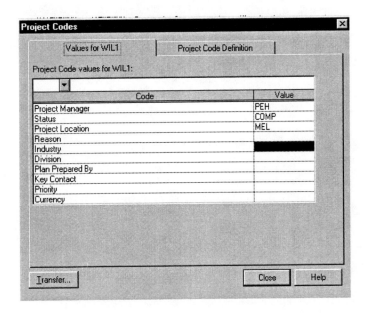

- Assign the Project Code values from the drop down box or

- Type in a value to create a new value.

- **Transfer** will allow you to copy the codes from another project.

24.10.3 Using Project Codes

Project Codes are used in the same way as Activity Codes and are listed at the bottom of the drop down lists when searching for them.

24.11 Primavera Post Office

This has some enhancements allowing you to:

- Display Expected Finish dates and

- Print Status Sheets.

24.12 Infomaker

P3 is supplied with the report writer **Infomaker**. With **Infomaker** you are able to produce a variety of text, graphical and chart reports.

25 ITEMS NOT COVERED IN THIS BOOK

The following subjects are not covered in this book.

- Statusing Project File, Send mail and File; receive mail.

- Report writing using Tools, Tabular Reports and Tools, Graphical Reports.

- Creating graphics using Primavera's graphics package Primavera Draw. This may be started with the program file **prmdraw.exe** found in the P3PROGS folder.

- Sharing project data with **ODBC** compliant software using **Tools**, **Update Data Dictionary**.

- The facility for summarizing up to 10 projects but leaving the project files intact using **Tools**, **Project Utilities**, **Summaries**.

- The facility for merging one or more projects into a host project to create one large project using **Tools**, **Project Utilities**, **Merge**.

- Primavera Post Office.

- P3 is supplied with a report writer **Infomaker**. With Infomaker you are able to produce a variety of text, graphical and chart reports.

Details of all these topics may be found in the User Manual and Help.

26 INDEX